Adapt *to* Thrive

"Adapting to new realities is difficult work. Yet, failing to adapt is a prescription for death. Beyond being (or finding) a better leader, beyond developing the next new program is the hard work of interior change. *Adapt to Thrive* helps us see the church not as organization but as organism and provides ten adaptations of interior changes needed in congregations today. We can easily see ourselves in the pages of Flowers and Vannoy's book—a real plus to help us talk about difficult things."

—Gil Rendle, senior consultant for the Texas Methodist Foundation and author of *Journey in the Wilderness* and *Back to Zero*

"I hope that all United Methodist pastors and local lay leaders will take seriously the ten cultural adaptations for the church outlined in this book. The authors vividly depict the changes that must occur in our local churches if we are to live into our mission to make disciples of Jesus for the transformation of the world. The anecdotes here will resonate with clergy and lay leaders as they illustrate how we are being called to authentic ministry with our neighbors, including those who are poor, marginalized, or suffering."

—Thomas G. Kemper, General Secretary, General Board of Global Ministries, The United Methodist Church

"The welding of deep insight with practical application is the hallmark of this insightful book. *Adapt to Thrive* empowers local churches and their leaders with a sound theological and organizational foundation. Presented here are ten concrete steps to move a congregation through the adaptation process and help guide them to engage the mission field. I commend this book to congregations and leaders who are hungering for new life in Christ!"

—Mike Lowry, Bishop, Central Texas Conference, The United Methodist Church

"*Adapt to Thrive* is filled with keen insights and stories from real congregations. This is a great resource for those who are willing to take on the challenge of reaching their neighbors with the grace and love of Jesus Christ."

—Craig Kennet Miller, Director of Congregational Development, General Board of Discipleship, The United Methodist Church

"Chock-full of stories that will preach and teach, this book encourages congregations to find missional identity, renewed purpose, and practices that align with that purpose. I recommend this book for churches who want to turn away from a decline into death to a renewal of life in Christ."

—Tex Sample, Robert B. and Kathleen Rogers Professor Emeritus of Church and Society, Saint Paul School of Theology

"This book is an excellent and practical map for the territory of congregational change. . . . Flowers and Vannoy have been there, done that, and lived to tell about it. This book will help you navigate real challenges with wisdom and humor. I recommend this book to clergy and laity who are committed to a hopeful future."

—Kim Cape, General Secretary, General Board of Higher Education and Ministry, The United Methodist Church

Adapt *to* Thrive

*How Your Church Must Identify Itself as a Unique Species,
Modify Its Dysfunctional Behaviors, and
Multiply Its Transformational Influence in Your Community*

John Flowers *and* Karen Vannoy

Abingdon Press
Nashville

ADAPT TO THRIVE:
HOW YOUR CHURCH MUST IDENTIFY ITSELF AS A UNIQUE SPECIES,
MODIFY ITS DYSFUNCTIONAL BEHAVIORS, AND MULTIPLY ITS
TRANSFORMATIONAL INFLUENCE IN YOUR COMMUNITY
Copyright © 2014 by Abingdon Press

This book is printed on acid-free paper.

Library of Congress Cataloging-in-Publication Data

Flowers, John, 1952–
    Adapt to thrive : how your church must identify itself as a unique species, modify its dysfunctional behaviors, and multiply its transformational influence in your community / John Flowers and Karen Vannoy.
        pages cm
    ISBN 978-1-4267-7303-7 (binding: pbk, adhesive perfect : alk. paper)
    1. Church renewal.   2. Change—Religious aspects—Christianity.   I. Vannoy, Karen.
II. Title.
    BV600.3.F57 2014
    253.dc23
                                                                        2013047675

14 15 16 17 18 19 20 21 22 23—10 9 8 7 6 5 4 3 2 1

MANUFACTURED IN THE UNITED STATES OF AMERICA

Contents

Preface – vii

Part One
Organizations, Organisms, and Christian Identity – 3
The Loss of Identity, and Missional Drift – 14

Part Two
Adapt to Your Unique Environment – 27
Survival of the Fittest – 30
The Need for Leaders – 36
Leaders Use the Power of Alignment – 42
Not All Churches Are Alike – 47

Part Three
Ten Cultural Adaptations for the Church – 53
Adaptation #1—From Scarcity to Abundance – 54
Adaptation #2—From Entitlement to Egalitarianism – 63
Adaptation #3—From Somberness to Playfulness – 68
Adaptation #4—From Limited Access to Trust – 72
Adaptation #5—From Ignoring the Neighbors to Embracing the Neighbors – 74
Adaptation #6—From Predictability to Freedom – 82
Adaptation #7—From Marginal Members to Deep Disciples – 87
Adaptation #8—From Baby Steps to Giant Leaps – 95
Adaptation #9—From Suspicion to Grace – 103
Adaptation #10—From a Generic Culture to a Self-Defined Culture – 107

Part Four
The Culture of Transformation – 115
Churches Can Practice Variance – 118
How Will We Know? – 122

Epilogue – 125
Appendix – 127

Preface

Most local churches appear to be headed for extinction. Thom Rainer, in his 2002 study of 1,159 churches, said that 94 percent of American churches are in decline. (One church administrator in southern California told us in private, "People are saying the churches which I supervise in this area are dying. That is incorrect; they are already dead.") Rainer points out that recent church attendance records show that in America, real attendance numbers are not near 40 percent as previously reported, but a shocking 17.7 percent ("Surprising Insights from the Unchurched," May 31, 2002, http:/www.bivocational.org/BIVO/data/unchurched.pdf).

Here are some statistics of just two mainline denominations from the Association of Religion Data Archives (ARDA):

United Methodist Church			
1968	41,901 churches	10,990,720 members	33,236 clergy
2005	34,397 churches	7,995,456 members	45,158 clergy

Evangelical Lutheran Church in America			
1987	11,133 churches	5,288,230 members	17,052 clergy
2006	10,470 churches	4,774,203 members	17,655 clergy

Ministry Matters, Aug. 7, 2012, "The Reason for a ReStart," by Dottie Escobedo Frank. Ministrymatters.com

The data from ARDA shows that thousands of local churches have gone extinct since 1968. These churches have disappeared because they were unable to adapt to the world around them. Some churches barely cling to life. These churches are staring at their own extinction but not because of predators or climate change. It is because of their failure to adapt. For congregations to survive, and then thrive, clergy and church leaders must adapt to new environments and cultures.

One member of a local church came into the sanctuary after the 9:00 a.m. contemporary service had concluded. The "postlude," prerecorded contemporary Christian music, was playing.

"Turn that music off!" she demanded. "It hurts my ears!"

"Well, then let's leave this place and go into the social hall," John said, hoping to redirect an eruption of negativity.

"I mean it," she continued, undeterred. "I experience physical pain from the volume of this music and I am sure these young people have hearing loss. We are responsible for that!"

"Doris," John offered, "You may well be correct, but I am not an audiologist. I don't know if we are contributing to hearing loss, but I do know that young people like this music played in worship at a volume that hurts your ears."

"I know what you are thinking," she continued. "You don't believe me when I say the music is painful to my ears."

"Doris," John replied (in his best "I love you but please don't tell me what I am thinking" voice), "I don't think anything of the sort. Here's what I think: If we don't build a worship service with music you find painful to your ears, then we will lose two or more generations of the church. If we don't adapt what we do and how we do it to the culture that surrounds us, then we will soon be just a memory and our building will be a museum."

Doris became that church's poster child for reluctant acquiescence. She was clearly not a fan of the music, but she wanted her church to survive long after she was gone.

The local church, whose experience is characterized by significant decline or plateau, has lost the skill with which we were formerly so blessed: the ability to adapt to a changing context. Adaptive leadership provides the best tools for equipping us to adapt to our current context. Just as important, adaptive leadership is the long-term path for our evolution through an unknown future. The business world understands the necessity of Adaptive Leadership. Other methods have been tried in the business world with only limited success. According to Jerry Thomas:

> Corporate leaders talk to their peers, copy their competitors, copy each other, and the theory becomes a managerial fad. Do any of these "canned" theoretical solutions really work? In some instances managerial theory or fad might work but for most businesses, the pursuit of theories and fads is a prescription for disaster and decay. ("Survival of the Fittest," *Decision Analyst*, http://www.decisionanalyst.com/publ_art/survival.dai)

The hard truth is that congregations lag far behind the secular world in making necessary adaptations. The secular world has adapted to technology while local churches are playing catch-up. Facebook, Twitter, and Skype have hit the business world and are even now giving way to newer forms of technology while in at least the last three congregations we served, 30 to 40 percent of the members did not even have an email account. Churches always seem to be one step behind the secular and business world in the learning curve. In the church we have tried all the theoretical solutions and canned practices.

What will be presented in this book is not a fad but a long-term look at the need for substantive change, and some immediate adaptations to help us meet the challenge. We will not be talking about things to do, but we will be talking about who we are. We will not spend time on gimmicks, but we will be examining identity. We will be talking about adapting to a new local church culture that is in alignment with both the local church's identity and unique ministry situation.

Business leaders already know what many of us in the local church still need to understand:

> The company and/or brand best "fitted" or best "adapted" to its environment (its markets, its customers) is most likely to survive, and

most likely to flourish. It means that companies or brands not well "fitted" to their markets will not survive long-term. (Thomas, "Survival of the Fittest")

In part 1, we identify Christians as a new species. In part 2, we identify every environment as unique from all others. In part 3, we will name ten cultural adaptations their local churches must make to be faithful for ministry in our unique settings. We will explore possible mutations and variations of the same species called Christians for the sake of ministry in unique settings. In part 4, we will identify how the new culture produces transformation. The goal is for every local church to understand that its pathway is through adaptation in order to thrive.

Part One

Organizations, Organisms, and Christian Identity

For decades we have been operating with an understanding of local churches as organizations. This knowledge has allowed us to benefit from a multidisciplinary approach to our problems. For example, organizational theory put us on the road to identifying best practices for church work. There are some things that each local church has in common with every other local church and some steps for implementing best practices that are common to all. Best practices enable us to acknowledge that the purpose of every local church is "to make new disciples of Jesus for the transformation of the world." Best practices demand that we practice self-definition. Best practices mean every healthy, thriving local church must be in alignment with that purpose. Yet we do not want best practices to simply be an attachment we make to the "latest thing" or the newest managerial fad. These hoped-for new behaviors come and go but never truly tackle our local church culture. For environmental adaptations (best practices) to be successful, the church must first make a series of major cultural adaptations. Cultural adaptations address the shift a church must make in attitude if it desires to be relevant to those beyond its doors. Once a church determines its desire (and adapts its culture) to be relevant, environmental adaptations focus the church on how to be relevant in its ministry setting and to its target population. To adopt best practices without the cultural shift will only produce limited results or even failure.

Adaptive leadership is another idea to come from organizational theory, and its applicability to our current situation provides us a new path to understand our past as well as our future. Our need for adaptation in order to thrive recognizes our unique settings for ministry. So, although best practices suggest that in some ways all local churches are alike, organizational theory of adaptation acknowledges that every local church is unique, with differences in environment, history, and culture, and must adapt in accordance with these elements in order to thrive. How we adapt to new cultures and environments will determine our ability to thrive as the church for tomorrow.

We can learn a lot by understanding church as an organization, but organizational theory is not the only discipline from which we can learn. The late Dr. Edwin Friedman, rabbi and clinical therapist from Bethesda, Maryland, observed that congregations behaved like living organisms. Dr. Friedman is credited with bringing family systems theory to bear on life inside a congregation. Family systems theory helps counselors, treatment programs, and therapists to understand individual behaviors inside the family. As a simple example, imagine your own family of origin as a mobile, with each member of the family represented by a different object on the mobile.

Through family systems theory we learn that when one member of the family changes (one object on the mobile moves), then the entire family changes as well (the whole mobile moves). The family's corresponding movement may serve simply to restore equilibrium or represent something more, an adaptation to the change another family member initiates. Because we are living organisms, we have strong abilities to change and adapt to our environments, not just when we are young, but throughout our lives. The change in members of a congregation, especially the leaders of a congregation, will have a ripple effect throughout the church. In some ways the rippling is unpredictable, but through family systems theory, we can begin to understand how these adaptations can end stagnation and give rise to renewal.

When we think of local churches as organisms—living, breathing entities, a natural next step is to examine the ways adaptation fends off extinction. Living organisms utilize adaptive leadership; it provides direction for the ways organisms can survive in new environments. Observation of adaptation in the physical world gives us a new way of understanding how adaptation can work inside the local church.

Observation of adaptation in the physical world gives us a new way of understanding how adaptation can work inside the local church.

Identity: Remember to Whom You Belong

Every reader of this book has seen a finch. Finches exist in all parts of the globe and are one of the most common birds. Yet the finch is a unique bird, just as a Christian is a unique human being. What kind of adaptations did the finch make to ensure its survival and ability to thrive in so many varied settings? What kinds of adaptations have Christians made to ensure their ability to survive? What kinds of adaptations will Christians need to make in the future? The answer to these questions begins with an understanding of God's created world.

Charles Darwin not only teaches us to identify species, but he teaches us that new variations in species have the potential to appear all the time. In his pursuit to understand the environment of the Galapagos Islands, Darwin found many new kinds of animal life and discovered how each of these were adapted to variable conditions on the islands. When we understand Darwin's observations about species, adaptations, and variances inside evolutionary theory, we can better understand the adaptive opportunities and challenges of Christians, denominations, and even local church ministries. That may sound like an incredible leap, but consider this: Experts in biodiversity say that in 2010 there were 200 to 400 billion birds on our planet. Obviously, not all birds are the same, so we divide them into different groups and categorize them by various characteristics. Scientists believe there are nine to ten thousand species of birds on our planet. The variety and number of differences between birds is astonishing, and yet they all share some characteristics. A seagull is not an eagle and a penguin is not a parrot, though all birds have wings. The wings are different shapes and sizes. Size varies and size matters, yet all birds have wings.

It is also true that within the human species, there are both myriad differences and absolutely consistent characteristics. These differences and consistencies extend even to our human belief systems. Every individual person believes in something. Just like the wings of a bird, belief comes in different shapes and sizes. There is belief in God, belief in karma, belief in one's own personal power, belief in country. There are at least as many different beliefs as there are different wings on birds, at least as many different belief systems among human beings as there are different species of birds on our planet. Of those nine to ten thousand (maybe more) belief systems, experts believe there are twenty-two major religions (belief systems) in the world. The top four religious belief systems by number—Christianity, Islam, Buddhism, and Hinduism—have approximately five billion followers ("Major Religions of the World Ranked by Number of Adherents," 2005; adherents.com).

On the Galapagos Islands Darwin saw thousands of birds, yet there was a particular bird that drew his attention: the finch. On Galapagos, Darwin collected what he thought were three different species of finch, each unique to three different islands. Some two years after his return from his world tour, when examining his specimens more closely, he discovered that the three specimens he collected in his travels were actually the same species of finch. He found at least three different adaptations of the common finch. The finch on one island had a long, slender beak to drink nectar from flowers. On another island, the finch had a mid-size beak better suited for eating insects. On still another island, the finch had a shorter, stronger beak for cracking seeds open to get at the meat inside. Each adaptation of finch had a different beak though they all came from the Galapagos Islands chain (Michael Jackson, *Galápagos: A Natural History*).

On another island, the finch had a mid-size beak better suited for eating insects.

Christianity is like the finch family. We are all one species. We can look very different from one another (and do), so much so that one might not even recognize another as Christian! Yet for all our variances, we are the same species. When Christianity first began to spread without the benefit of an organization, there were many different beliefs and practices, each suited to the community in which the church arose. By the time we became the state religion of the Holy Roman Empire, we were well on our way to becoming an organization. To be an organization is not a bad thing; it was probably in the church's case a good and necessary thing. The Catholic Church has survived for two thousand years, outlasting scores of different governments. What other authoritative body can say that? And the church has managed to duplicate itself across the globe and onto virtually every continent. Organizations are good at duplication. Some would say it's what they do best.

Although there is some documentation of organisms that have actually duplicated, most organisms are not adept at duplication. This is certainly true of humans—so much so that every human being is unique. (Just ask a twin!) So, while cloning is unnatural for us, adaptation comes to us more easily. As newborns, our adaptation begins when we leave the womb and take that first gulp of air. We grow as individuals only because we know how to adapt. Consider all the ways you have adapted in order to live and grow and thrive throughout your life. Yet when we humans are gathered into organizations, stagnation can take hold, and we become ever more devoted to duplication, replicating and transplanting our systems, methods, preferences, and practices, and even our culture, wherever they will take root. This has certainly been true for the church. Can congregations learn to adapt to their environments like the varieties of finches adapted their beaks to their unique food source? Just like the finch, we must adapt to thrive.

7

Can congregations learn to adapt to their environments like the varieties of finches adapted their beaks to their unique food source?

Christians Are the Finches of All Birds

Just as finches share some qualities with other birds, all human beings share common traits with every other mammal. Mammals have hair, three middle-ear bones, mammary glands in females, a circulatory system with a four-chambered heart, and a neocortex (a region of the brain). Still, we remember that finches are a unique species of bird, and human beings are a unique species of mammal.

All finches have twelve tail feathers, four primary feathers, and strong gliding skills. If you see these three characteristics in a bird, you have found a finch. We identify different species by their key characteristics. Identity flows out of these key characteristics, and *an organism's adaptation does not have to change its identity.*

All Christians are disciples of Jesus Christ, celebrate sacraments, and, whether or not it is a bodily resurrection or the resurrection faith, all Christians believe in some form of resurrection. If you see these characteristics in someone's belief system, you have found a Christian.

Once a Finch, Always a Finch

We are Christians, not better than any other religious believers of the world, but different, distinguishable from all other believers. We are a different species, distinctive from our Muslim brothers and sisters, who, in turn, are a different species, distinct from our Buddhist companions. Believers of all faiths live all over the world, and increasingly live in the same places, together. So, our distinction as

Christians is not defined by our habitat. Our distinction, and the distinction of all religions, perhaps, is best characterized by our purpose. The purpose of all Christians is to "*make disciples of Jesus Christ for the transformation of the world*." This is our identity. This is how we define ourselves. Just as the finch would be lost trying to be a parrot, we are lost when we forget to whom we belong. This is how we see ourselves. We are Christians, followers of Jesus.

John's Story

In the beginning I was taught differently. Just like many of you, my parents shaped my identity, particularly my father. I recall one standard Friday night as a teenager in my family. I had a movie date with a girl from school. Since my curfew was 11:00 p.m., unusually early for a seventeen-year-old, I thought, I preferred to catch an early movie so my date and I could spend some quality time together afterwards. The last step before going out the door was to receive the keys to the car from my father. Stepping into his room, I let him know it was time.

"I'm leaving now, Dad," I said. "Can I have the car keys?"

My father then fumbled in his pocket until he found the keys, took them out, and put them in my hand, but he was not yet ready to turn loose the keys. And so we would do a little dance. I would pull the keys toward me, and he would pull back and ask: "What movie are you going to?"

"I don't know and I don't care," I replied.

"Do you have money?" he inquired.

"I can always use more," was my standard response.

"Here's five dollars. That should hold you through the night's activities," he said.

With both of us holding fast to the keys, he reached in his pocket with his free hand, pulled out a $5 bill, and gave it to me.

"Is there anything else?" I asked, with a smile on my

9

face, knowing full well that there was something else. That something else was the last thing he always told me before I left the house to go on a date. It was something his father had told him years before and my grandfather's father had told him. It was the most important thing a young man could hear as he entered the sometimes confusing, always complex world of trying on relationships. He would not fully release the keys until he told me.

"Remember who you belong to."

I knew immediately what he was saying. No explanation was needed. In his eyes and in mine, I belonged to a group of people who were polite to all adults and who treated girls with dignity and respect. I belonged to a people who would not break traffic laws, or any laws for that matter, and who would honor curfews (hard to do since my curfew was 11:00 p.m., and my date could stay out until midnight), and who would never, ever, ever do anything to embarrass my people.

Strong in my memory is when my brother violated my father's sense of family identity. My father had to travel some distance to the location of my brother's serious transgression. In the moment that my father first saw my brother, there was no yelling. There were no angry outbursts or threats. Apparently the announcement of punishment would have to wait because, for my dad, first things first. He sat down next to my brother, gathered himself, and with sadness in his voice said, "This is not who we are." If he had not realized it up until that time, in that moment, my brother knew the seriousness of his offense.

"Remember who you belong to" stuck with John over the years, and he used it with his own sons as they were growing up. Those conversations with his father propelled him into academic, personal, and professional reflections. Who am I? Who do I truly belong to? and How do I see myself? prove to be helpful questions for growing self-awareness and establishing identity.

Feral Children

Feral children help us understand that our identity is more mal-leable, less fixed, than the identity of the finch. A feral child is a human child who has lived isolated from human contact from a very young age, and has no (or little) experience of human care, loving or social behavior, and, crucially, of human language. Accounts of feral children are tragic stories of persons who, through no fault of their own, do not know who they belong to. Due to their isolation from their species, feral children lose their identity. Raised by a different species of mammal, these children have not had human behavior modeled for them and do not know how to be human.

Rudyard Kipling draws a fictional account of Mowgli, a feral child in the novel *The Jungle Book*, but there are true accounts of how human identity can be blurred, marred, or even forgotten in feral children. Depending on which resource is consulted, there have been at least ten cases of feral children in history. Survival in the wild while being raised by animals is truly a miracle. Yet reentry into a world of human beings is extremely traumatic. Feral children do not have the most basic social and behavioral skills. Feral children have been deprived of human identity and purpose.

Unlike feral children, the finch cannot change his or her kind. It is what it *is*, and the belonging is governed by instinct. Not so for human beings in general, and certainly not for Christians in particular. We can and regularly do forget or forsake who we are.

Choosing to Be the New Creation

John's inquiry expands from these individual or familial questions of identity into his basic identity as a Christian. He is still connected to the people named Flowers, but his self-definition is even more closely bound to his identity as a disciple of Jesus Christ. Whereas he still honors his father and carries the family name, he now belongs to the species called Christians first, and the species called Flowers second.

What if we were to think of Christians as a distinctive species of human beings? What if we were to think of all local churches as communities of people whose primary definition is not from the species they were born into but as a new species, people who follow Jesus Christ? In Jesus' encounter with Nicodemus, "born again" was the language used, and the metaphor reflects that when we profess faith in Jesus Christ, we are then transformed by adaptation into a new species. This new creation has a new identity, and we spend our lives adapting to what that means for us.

What if we were to think of all Christians as defined by their primary and distinctive purpose—to make new disciples of Jesus Christ for the transformation of the world? Jesus wants us to belong to him, even if our adaptation means we have to leave our families of origin. Found in all three synoptic gospels (Mark 3, Matthew 12:48b-50, and Luke 9:23) is Jesus' instruction of what it means to be a Christian: Say no to yourself, take up your cross daily, and follow him.

Whether Jesus came to make a unique variation on Judaism or to forge a new species altogether, we can agree on this clear distinction: Believers in Jesus are students of Jesus (disciples), who become radically transformed through following him. Many Christian communities bear witness to our becoming a new creation at the point of conversion or baptism. Saul of Tarsus took the new name Paul as a symbol of his new identity. As a pastor, Karen always asks the parents of an infant presented for baptism, "What name shall be given to this child?" When we baptize adults, we ask, "With what name do you wish to be baptized?" These are ways that we symbolize the adaptation from a family of origin into the family of Christians. It is the way we remember whose family we belong to: the Christian family.

A barrier to gaining clarity in our self-definition as a species of humans called Christians has been our tendency to think of all local churches as organizations rather than organisms. Local churches are more than just organizations. Local churches also behave like organisms, living, breathing, and evolving. This runs deep in our Judeo-Christian life. In Exodus when Moses encounters the burning bush at Horeb (the mountain of God), he asks God a question: "Who are you?"

"If I now come to the Israelites and say to them, 'The God of your ancestors has sent me to you,' they are going to ask me, 'What's this God's name?' What am I supposed to say to them?"

God said to Moses, "I Am Who I Am. So say to the Israelites, 'I Am has sent me to you.'" (Exodus 3:13-14)

While the exact meaning of God's name is unknown, through the centuries it has been translated different ways. The Common English Bible says "I Am Who I Am" but other translators might translate this phrase as "I Am Who I Was" or "I Am Who I Am Becoming." Even God's name communicates a God who is adapting to the unique environments of God's people. We worship a God who leads an adaptive faith.

We worship a God who leads an adaptive faith.

God sent Adam and Eve out of the garden of Eden but dressed them and provided fertile land for them to farm. God gave a covenant in Exodus and later wrote a new covenant on the hearts of the people. The God who commanded that no graven images ever be made came to earth in a human body, as Jesus. All of these are adaptations. This imaginative way of seeing God opens our eyes to a new, imaginative way of seeing the local Christian congregation.

The local church is not intended to be static or fixed. To the contrary, our species is an adaptive organism living out its purpose. When we remember who we truly belong to—a God who is still and always *becoming*, and a Savior who adapted his teachings to meet people where they found themselves—then we are able to understand adaptation as the state of being for our corporate life together. The becoming God reminds us that churches are organisms *as well as* organizations.

The Loss of Identity, and Missional Drift

In our experience of local congregations as well as denominational entities, we are good at behaving like organizations. We create hierarchies, protocols, and practices. We easily assume the purpose of a comfortable organization that practices inclusivity, drinks coffee together, talks about God, and often srves as a social service agency. This is not in alignment with our given purpose, to make new disciples of Jesus Christ for the transformation of the world, yet is a model that has been duplicated throughout North America. As with all other organizations, local churches, when stressed, will solidify, institutionalize, retreat, and decline. Like all organisms, local churches will adapt or die. It is easy to get off track. Some call this a missional drift.

Peter Steinke writes in the article "Avoiding Mission Drift":

> Limping along without a focus is called *mission drift*. It is what happens when people come together to support an objective but forget what the objective is. People lose their reason for being, even though they go through the motions. (http://www.alban.org/conversation.aspx?id=9167)

Missional drift means we have drifted away from our true definition and purpose; we begin to operate under a different set of assumptions and guidelines.

For example, a Sunday-morning eye clinic was operating in the basement of one local church in Texas. The hour had come for weekly worship and the pastor instructed the workers to shut down operations. Someone in charge of that clinic pleaded, in the name of efficiency, "Please let us stay open one more hour. The need is so great and we will be able to see five more patients if we can operate the clinic until noon." The pastor listened with respect to his health care colleague but was firm in his response: "Never forget that we are a church that happens to have an eye clinic, we are not an eye clinic that happens to be located in a church."

The last church we served together named their vision, purpose, and journey. We spent a lot of sweat and energy to find the right words for the vision and journey, but we agreed in quick order that our purpose was to make disciples of Jesus Christ for the transformation of the world. We said it in a slightly different way—unite new faces with Jesus Christ—but it is essentially the same purpose held by all Christians. The church then decided to post the purpose on the wall for all to see.

> "I hope we do not make the letters permanent," one congregation member said.
>
> "What on earth do you mean?" another responded.
>
> "I am just saying that I would not want to attach it to the walls in a permanent way. I do not want to put up letters that cannot be changed in the future. Years from now we might vote to have a different purpose."
>
> "I understand that in the future our vision and journey might change," the respondent offered. "No one can know what the future holds, and we may need to try different ways to reach others in the name of Christ. Our purpose, however, will never change. It was given to us early on, in Matthew 28. Our purpose should be chiseled in stone."

Christians all over the world can be found living out their purpose of making disciples of Jesus for the transformation of the world. We are given that purpose in Matthew 28:18-19: "Jesus came near and spoke to them, 'I've received all authority in heaven and on earth. Therefore, go and make disciples of all nations, baptizing them in the name of the Father and of the Son and of the Holy Spirit.'"

At a Desert Southwest Urban Academy session in 2010, Doug Anderson, head of the Bishop Rueben Job Center and nationally known local church consultant, showed us that in Acts 1 Christians are given instructions for inclusive evangelism. "Rather, you will receive power when the Holy Spirit has come upon you, and you will be my witnesses in Jerusalem, in all Judea and Samaria, and to the end of the earth" (v. 8). Doug said, "You will be given the power to witness through the Holy Spirit in Jerusalem, which is where you are, in Judea, which is your home, in Samaria, and the world. Samaria and the world are the places where the disciples would find people not like themselves. We are called to make disciples of Jesus where we are, at home, and throughout the world."

To the extent that we have failed to follow our charge as found in Matthew 28 and Acts 1, we have failed to fulfill our purpose. We have forgotten to whom we truly belong. We have forgotten who we are as believers and our identity as a faith community.

How can we invite persons to a transforming church when we are not sure of our own identity and purpose? If we have been given our instructions on what to do and how to do it, why does it not get done? Part of the answer can be found in Paul's letter to the Romans: "I don't know what I'm doing, because I don't do what I want to do. Instead, I do the thing that I hate" (7:15).

It is not only the sin that lives in us that prevents us from fulfilling our purpose. It is also that we have forgotten who we belong to; we are as lost and confused as the people we would try to reach. Clergy and laity alike share the blame.

At a dinner party, we overheard the following conversation:

"I was passing by an elderly woman in the grocery store aisle as she reached for a cereal box on the display case. She meant to pull just one box down but ended up tipping over the entire display case."

"That is awful," one of the guests exclaimed. "What did you do?"

"I stood the display case back up in its original position, bent down, and began picking up the boxes and placing them back on the case," the man said.

"How long did that take?"

"Not long, five or ten minutes."

"That was very Christian of you."

From the kitchen came the voice of our hostess, who happened to be a clergywoman:

"How many times do I have to remind you? *Christian* is not a synonym for *nice*. It is good to be nice and thoughtful, and practice random or intentional acts of kindness, but that is not the Christian faith."

Many in our local churches continue to believe that Jesus commanded us to be nice. Many go to worship to learn how to be a nicer person. This is not what Jesus hoped for.

Christian is not a synonym for *nice.*

Others believe that being a good Christian means abstinence from alcohol: "Lips that touch wine shall never touch mine." One man, responding to the question "Why do you go to church?" replied, "I need to collect stars for my crown."

Our favorite, though, was the elderly man who lived in a small town and had never attended worship since he was a kid. All of a sudden he shows up in worship one Sunday morning, then the next Sunday too, and the next, and then the following Sunday as well. On his fifth Sunday of regular worship attendance, the pastor found the opportunity to ask the question:

"Why have you started attending worship after all these years?"

His pragmatic response came without hesitation. "I decided to cram for my finals."

This older adult reminds us that thousands of persons attend worship regularly so they can get to heaven. The confusion over our purpose as Christians bleeds over into a confusion for many as to why they attend church.

True, many folks who attend worship every week are not focused on heaven, but they are still not sure why they keep coming to church. These folks are "Blenders," as identified by Gabe Lyons in his book *The Next Christians.* Lyons explains that Blenders inherited their parent's religion. The faith of Blenders is a byproduct of family identity and not always a personal decision. Blenders are particularly attracted to churches whose highest value is to create acceptance. For these churches, creating acceptance trumps making disciples of Jesus for the transformation of the world. Perhaps the local church that attracts Blenders feels more familiar and comfortable, like a favorite pillow or winter coat.

The deeper meaning for the gospel, the urgency of our task, is lost as we "play church" rather than "be the church." Wayne Jacobsen, who attends many different local church worship services in a year's time, says that although many congregations are playing church, some remember who they belong to. The local churches that remember who they belong to are "being the church" ("Why I Don't Go to Church Anymore," Wayne Jacobsen, Lifestream Ministries, 2001):

> I visit a couple of dozen different congregations a year that I find are more centered on relationship than religion. Jesus is at the center of their life together, and those who act as leaders are true servants and not playing politics of leadership. All are encouraged to minister to one another. I pray that even more of them (local churches) are renewed in a passion for Jesus, a genuine concern for each other, and a willingness to serve the world with God's love. But I think we'd have to admit that these are rare in our communities, and many only last for a short span before they unwittingly look to institutional answers for the needs of the body instead of remaining dependent on Jesus.

It is tough to admit that too many churches have forgotten three essential things:

1. Who we belong to.

2. Our self-definition (our DNA) as followers of Jesus.

3. Our purpose: to make new disciples of Jesus for the transformation of the world.

Gil Rendle is a helpful voice in sorting out the kind of species we need to be. Rendle suggests that previously, the desired output of local churches was to maintain happy congregations and satisfied pastors. This output, as Rendle identifies it, is at least outdated and, he would contend, unfaithful to the gospel. Rendle identifies the new species of Jesus followers as people who differentiate from historic outputs of happy congregations and satisfied pastors. The output of local church adaptive leadership is now making new disciples of Jesus for the transformation of the world. Our species is Jesus followers, not just Jesus worshipers (*Faith and Leadership*, "What If We Have Too Much?" Sept. 28, 2010).

Adapting from our familty species of Flowers or Vannoy or Smith or Jones, and so on, into a species of Christians means everything is different. Our self-identity is no longer in our biological family. Jesus gave us warning that the difficult task of adapting meant redefining who we are and who we are becoming.

> His mother and brothers arrived. They stood outside and sent word to him, calling for him. A crowd was seated around him, and those sent to him said, "Look, your mother, brothers, and sisters are outside looking for you."
>
> He replied, "Who is my mother? Who are my brothers?" Looking around at those seated around him in a circle, he said, "Look, here are my mother and my brothers. Whoever does God's will is my brother, sister, and mother." (Mark 3:31-35)

Jesus was calling (and is still calling) for us to adapt to this new self-definition called Christian. The process of adaptation is difficult and demanding. Adaptation as a new species, called Christian, requires going back to the very beginning. We must be born anew.

Nicodemus was not yet ready to leave the lens given to him by his birth family, even though he was fascinated with the miraculous signs from this man of God. He may have begun a process of adaptation into a believer, a follower of Jesus, but he had a long way to go before he could be reborn as a Christian, as told in John 3.

> There was a Pharisee named Nicodemus, a Jewish leader. He came to Jesus at night and said to him, "Rabbi, we know that you are a teacher who has come from God, for no one could do these miraculous signs that you do unless God is with him."
>
> Jesus answered, "I assure you, unless someone is born anew, it's not possible to see God's kingdom."
>
> Nicodemus asked, "How is it possible for an adult to be born? It's impossible to enter the mother's womb for a second time and be born, isn't it?"(vv. 1-4)

Nicodemus was certain that no one could climb back into his or her mother's womb and go through the birth process one more time. It is physically impossible. What was Jesus trying to say? Nicodemus was saying, "We cannot literally accomplish what you are asking us to do!"

Maybe Jesus was saying "you belong to a new species now." For himself, he knew he could not go back to Nazareth and make everything the way it was when he was young. We cannot turn back the clock. What Jesus is saying is more than John the Baptist's message of repentance. Being different from who we were before is not enough. He is saying that we need to adapt and become a completely new species, one of the Jesus followers rather than a species defined by our biological origins.

Being different from who we were before is not enough.

Jesus answered [Nicodemus's question], "I assure you, unless someone is born of water and the Spirit, it's not possible to enter God's kingdom. Whatever is born of the flesh is flesh, and whatever is born of the Spirit is spirit. Don't be surprised that I said to you, 'You must be born anew.' God's Spirit blows wherever it wishes. You hear its sound, but you don't know where it comes from or where it is going. It's the same with everyone who is born of the Spirit."

Nicodemus said, "How are these things possible?" (John 3:5-9)

Once we become Christians, our old life purpose is obsolete. We have a new purpose given to us, to make new disciples of Jesus for the transformation of the world. Our adaptation to that new purpose will take us a lifetime. At first, learning that we belong to God is intriguing and attractive. We run forward into a new life. Taking more steps toward redefinition, our pace tends to slow as we encounter the depth of the changes needed to adapt to our new identity.

We may even come to a stop, unwilling to go further because we love our comforts. Doug Anderson reports that, "As lay leaders we often stop at the border of comfort and preference" (Urban Academy Desert Southwest Conference UMC, Sept. 24–25, 2010). Anderson reflects on Jesus' instruction to the young man who seeks salvation in Matthew 19: "Jesus said, 'If you want to be complete, go, sell what you own, and give the money to the poor. Then you will have treasure in heaven. And come follow me'" (v. 21). But when the young man heard this, he went away saddened, because he had many possessions and was too comfortable with his worldly possessions to become a new disciple of Jesus for the transformation of the world. His personal preference was to retain his possessions and proclaim his love for Jesus, but, as we see, that is not possible. The young man must be born again. The young man must remember that it is God whom he belongs to, not his biological family and certainly not his possessions.

The first step in the born-anew adaptation as a new species is to recognize that your life is not about what you want, what you need, or what you desire, but for your species your life is all about what Jesus wants, needs, and desires. We are to put self-interest on the back burner. We are to deny ourselves. It is not about you; it is about following Jesus.

> Jesus said to everyone, "All who want to come after me must say no to themselves, take up their cross daily, and follow me. All who want to save their lives will lose them. But all who lose their lives because of me will save them. What advantage do people have if they gain the whole world for themselves yet perish or lose their lives?" (Luke 9:23-26)

What will people give in exchange for their lives? This is a difficult question. We are willing to give up some things, maybe even most things, but to give up everything is a bit much. We have all heard the rationales and spin doctoring that accompany most stewardship campaigns:

"I give some of my annual income to the church, but I also give to other things, like the symphony, and my child's school, and political campaigns. Surely God does not expect me to give a whole ten percent to church. How much does God really expect me to give up?"

The answer is, everything. If we are adapting as a new species, from a family identity into a follower of Jesus, then we are expected to give extravagantly and sacrificially. There are no exceptions.

The second step is "take up your cross." This means, according to Doug Anderson, to engage the world outside of our comfort zone. "Take up your cross" means doing what makes us uncomfortable for the purpose of making new disciples of Jesus in order that the world will be transformed.

Many theologians have postulated that the suffering from a "thorn in the flesh" described by Paul was not a physical ailment. Perhaps it was an emotional limitation, or a difficult church parishioner. But for many of us, the thorn is the profound discomfort of moving outside our comfort zones into relationships that make us uncomfortable. Like the old Star Trek line says, we, as disciples, are called "to boldly go where no man has gone before." New and scary places cause us great trepidation and anxiety; therefore, they are the thorns in our flesh.

The third step is "follow me." In other words, be transformed as we continue in the ministry of transformation with others.

In our first book, *Not Just a One Night Stand: Ministry with the Homeless*, we wrote about how one deeply committed disciple of Jesus asked for help in his own struggle with a thorn in his flesh.

"I want to be in ministry with persons who are desperately poor and come to eat breakfast on Sunday morning at our church. I know that means to go beyond simply serving the meal but it means to eat with them and have conversation with them, to be in relationship with them. I want all that, but I confess I am not sure how to do it. How do I engage in conversation with our brothers and sisters from the street?"

"Go and find someone who is sitting by themselves and eating alone," began one who himself had entered the thorn in the flesh world and found fulfillment in ministry with homeless persons. "Take your tray of food and start out something like this: 'This is scary for me. I confess I would like for us to have a conversation together, but I don't know how to get it started. Would you be so kind as to let me know something about yourself? Where did you sleep last night? Do you feel safe sleeping there? How long have you been on the streets? Where are the best places to catch a meal in this city? Where are you from? Do you keep in touch with your family? Do they know where you are?' If you ask questions like these, in this way, then you will do fine." Deep disciples find ways to treat all persons with dignity and respect. The church needs deeply-discipled Jesus followers. (Upper Room Press, 2009)

The Reverend Duane Zimmerman, pastor of a large Protestant church located in Arizona, preached a sermon using a profound image whose origin belongs to an unknown prophetic voice in the church of long ago. Duane suggested that Christian disciples are adapting. "For too long we have been admirers of Jesus when, in fact, we have been called to be followers of Jesus." Jesus followers are not chained to their possessions, are willing to make significant financial sacrifices, will connect with persons outside their comfort zone, and will follow Jesus wherever he leads.

Our future depends on us moving from one output to another. Our future depends on us moving from being admirers of Jesus to followers of Jesus. Our future depends on remembering whom we belong to. Our future is utterly dependent on our ability to live into and out of our designated purpose, to make new disciples of Jesus for the transformation of the world. To have a future means we must adapt to thrive. In the next two parts, we will address two different kinds of adaptations. Part 2 looks at environmental adaptations a church must make to connect to its neighbors. Part 3 looks at the typical cultural adaptations necessary for the environmental adaptations to work.

Our future depends on us moving from being admirers of Jesus to followers of Jesus.

Part Two

Adapt to Your Unique Environment

For at least twenty-five years, churches actually have been talking about adapting to their communities, even if the language of adaptation wasn't being used. There are many wonderful resources available to aid in that work, and there's a list to get you started at the end of this book. If the proper leadership is available, and the cultural adaptations in part 3 are already underway, this kind of adaptation is usually fun and exciting for churches. When considering what environmental adaptations to make, be sure to start with accurate demographic information like

- Age/employment of area residents; socioeconomics
- Church interest/preference of the neighborhood
- Ethnicity, gender, and sexual orientation
- Diversity present; marital status of residents
- Rural, urban, suburban, established, or transient community issues or concerns; businesses, schools, and so on

Using the demographic information collected, churches can begin to experiment with the necessary adaptations to reach their community. In essence, the church is adapting to change in the way it appears to its surrounding community.

Mice Do It

In searching for adaptation models for the church, we can see how other species vary or adapt to their changing environments and learn something from them.

In the Arizona high desert there are many rocks and many mice.

Mice are a mobile bunch in this environment as they chase after food. There are dark mice that live on dark rocks, and there are light mice that live on light rocks. If food disappears from the light rocks, a light-colored mouse must move to an area of dark rocks to search for food to eat. However, the light mouse is highly visible to predators once he moves to the dark rocks unless his coat turns dark. The converse is true as well of dark mice on white rocks. Dark mice are vulnerable if their food source moves over to the light rocks. Coyotes and birds of prey can see the contrast of their fur against the rocks, and the nonadaptive mice are easy to pick off.

Some churches have lamented that the world is passing them by and they do not have the capacity to adapt to new ways. On one hand, this may be a simple, direct prophetic word and the process of decline toward extinction for mainline denominations may be irrevocable. On the other hand, maybe some churches are simply like mice trying to find food on the wrong rocks. DNA studies have shown that the color of a mouse's fur can change and that adaptation of color to match the environment's rock color will raise the probability of survival. In some cases, such adaptation could take generations. But human beings in general, and Christians in particular, are potentially more adaptive than that. Why can't local churches maintain their stated purpose while adapting their coat to the color of their environment? (In Darwinian language, this DNA adaptation is called mutation.)

Some churches have lamented that the world is passing them by and they do not have the capacity to adapt to these new ways.

Sean B. Carroll from the University of Wisconsin-Madison reports that "mutation produces variation" ("Rock Pocket Mice," 2013,

http://learn.genetics.utah.edu/content/selection/comparative/).
In other words, we have the same species, mice, but they have
changed color or adapted to a new environment. Local churches
must choose to be either light mice on dark rocks with their futures
in peril or light mice adapting quickly on dark rocks. The former is
doomed and the latter has the best chance to survive and thrive.

This adaptation speaks to our need to change the way we appear
to our neighbors. To do that, you have to know how your neighbors perceive you, and that would mean actually surveying your own
neighborhood. Many churches across the country have done just
that, with varying degrees of success. We've never read one account,
though, that said the gathering of the information was a waste of
time. Your denomination may gather some demographic information
for you (United Methodists do). If not, other demographic services
can supply you with information about the age, marital status, educa-
tional and income levels, and gender and ethnicity of your neighbors,
as well as their interest in religion. Check with your local city govern-
ment and Chamber of Commerce to see what information they routinely collect. This type of information is helpful, but won't tell you
how your church is perceived. One church we know obtained phone
lists for a five-mile radius around their church, and volunteers did
straight cold-calling. They were amazed how many people talked to
them and were candid in their responses. They learned the church was
perceived as upper income, elitist, traditional, older, unwelcoming to
minorities, and closed to anything but heterosexual orientation. This
was a reality check for the church—they had considered themselves
progressive and, well, "hip" for a church. They learned to take some
new directions after the survey in order to adapt their ministries so
that the could reach their neighbors.

The internet is full of resources on why younger generations are
not interested in church. Answers to this question have been heav-
ily surveyed and researched. Responses are predictable and mirror
the unchurched attitude toward organized religion in general. The
church is seen as hypocritical, judgmental, rule bound, out of touch
with issues regarding human sexuality and sexual orientation, exclusive, not concerned about social justice issues, too political, and so

on. The example of how rock mice adapt teaches us our need to adapt how we appear to others if we are to thrive.

Survival of the Fittest

Here are two important ideas from Darwin that add to our understanding of adaptation:

1. Species change over time.

2. The struggle to survive will not only occur between species but also between individuals within the same species.

Jerry Thomas writes about Darwin's learning:

By "survival of the fittest" Darwin did not mean that the toughest will survive, the swiftest will win, the smartest will succeed, or the biggest will dominate. What Darwin meant was something far different. Darwin said that the organism that best "fits" its environment had the best chance of survival; hence the term "survival of the fittest." The plant or animal [or local church by extrapolation] best "fitted" to its natural environment, according to the theory, would be the most likely to survive and thrive. ("Survival of the Fittest," *Decision Analyst*, http://www.decisionanalyst.com/publ_art/survival.dai)

The organism that best fits its environment has the best chance of survival. In the most simple of terms, if your church is located in Phoenix, Arizona, it is not a good idea to have a noon-time, outdoor, end-of-summer celebration in late August or September, when the temperature is guaranteed to top 110 degrees in the shade. But a casual, seasonal gathering in September is a good idea for families, so local churches in Phoenix that want to survive and thrive must practice fitness for their natural environment. In Phoenix, hold your "Get Back in Pocket" celebration indoors, in air-conditioned space, with ice cream and cookies. Maybe have a waterslide on the church lawn for the kids. This would have the additional benefit of community members driving by and hearing their kids say, "Daddy, Mommy, that looks like fun, I want to go to a church like that!"

If your church is located in North Dakota, fitness for that local environment would suggest an outdoor August or September gathering works fine. However, you may want to avoid walking through the neighborhood for Christmas caroling. Fingers are too cold to hold the sheet music, and people nestled in front of their fireplaces are not eager to open their doors to better hear the music and honor your effort. I can just hear the living room conversation as the carolers move on to the next house:

"Frankie, why did you open that door?" asks Fred, who is headed for the closet to retrieve his overcoat.

"They are from the church down the street," answers Frankie, always the one to do the polite thing. "They are nice people, and I didn't want to be rude."

"They are idiots who cannot read a thermometer," replies grumpy, and now freezing, Fred. "Bet they all lose feeling in their toes before the Jones's house at the end of the street."

Christmas caroling doesn't have to be abandoned in North Dakota. The churches that survive and thrive simply go to nursing homes or sing in the fellowship hall or activity center with hot cider, apple pie, and white elephant gifts. This is an appropriate adaptation to the natural environment called North Dakota!

Weather is the easiest environmental factor to acknowledge when adapting our behavior to survive and thrive. It can govern not only how we reach people, but opportunities for new mission as well. One church in San Antonio realized that their city's large homeless population was stressed beyond reason when the temperature dropped. The overflow for local shelters exceeded capacity. A lay leader began a system where persons who happened to be homeless were invited to sleep inside the church on cold winter nights.

It was an easy system. Volunteers were recruited to come and supervise the slumber party during those cold nights. Other volunteers who were unable to stay the night provided food and drink. Hot cocoa, decaf coffee, and sandwiches were prepared and ready. An announcement was made to put it all in motion: "If the weather forecasters report that the overnight temperatures will drop below freezing, then come to the church."

31

Soon the word spread within the homeless community. Volunteers at the church began to build relationships with persons who slept with the stars as their roof. Word went out, "If it is below 32 degrees, then come." But soon after, it became "if it is below 40 degrees."

The church leaders adapted from the mind-numbing boredom of quiet time for everyone into some intentional faith development activities. Prayer group time and Bible study were added. What started out as a simple adaptation to freezing temperatures grew into a profound ministry of making new disciples of Jesus for the transformation of the world.

These church leaders were now being transformed from their previous cold-weather ministry. More persons who had a heart for the poor came to join in the ministry, and these new seekers began to attend worship. Further adaptations, too many to name, appeared as the established church leaders listened to the needs of the desperately poor. This congregation began to thrive. Sadly, another congregation not more than two blocks away made no effort to adapt. It is now on its last legs.

In addition to adaptations for weather, we see the necessity to adapt to our neighborhoods. One church in a changing neighborhood tells the story of many. Fifty years ago this neighborhood was 98 percent Anglo. Today the neighborhood is 78 percent Latino. Fifty years ago the local church membership was 95 percent Anglo. Today, the local church membership is 95 percent Anglo. The membership decline has gone on for fifty years. There has been no adaptation of that local church to its natural environment. Adaptation is not even on its radar. When asked, "What do you want in a pastor?" there was prolonged silence. Finally, a longtime member rose to say, "We want a pastor to hold worship on Sunday morning, visit us in the hospital, and bury our dead." We appreciate that lay member's honesty, but:

1. That is not the purpose of the church.

2. This nonadaptive approach will in effect put the church on a ventilator and feeding tube, producing nothing but a slow, lingering death.

3. It is a scandalous misuse of resources.

Darwin says there is intense competition for limited resources; in other words, to revisit the bird analogy, there are a lot of finches out there trying to survive, and there are lots of local churches out there trying to survive.

The most "fit" finches, the ones that have the best adaptation (mutation or variation), will survive. Mission, vision, purpose, or journey statements are simply an answer to an outsider's request to learn more about your congregation. These local church declarations about the how, what, when, where, and why of making new disciples of Jesus for the transformation of the world is what identifies the unique adaptation/variance for that local church. A healthy church is not only dependent upon its ability to adapt but also on its ability to understand the adaptations it has made to thrive.

Often we see slogans printed in bulletins, on websites, and even on the walls of the local church itself. Travis Park UMC in San Antonio lives out "unconditional love and justice in action." Church of the Resurrection in Kansas City aims to "build a community where nonreligious and nominally religious people are becoming deeply committed Christians." Glide in San Francisco proclaims itself "a radically inclusive, just, and loving community mobilized to alleviate suffering and break the cycles of poverty and marginalization." One church in Phoenix has adapted local church life to "uniting our lives with God's dream for the world." Ask any member of that congregation, What is God's dream for the world? and they will quickly answer, "Thy kingdom come, thy will be done on earth as it is in heaven."

These four healthy, adaptive mission statements separate each church from the crowd of Sunday morning offerings in their geographic areas. Contrast them with a nonadaptive mission statement such as "We are the friendly church in the heart of the city." This does not touch or even point to the church's purpose and could be the mission statement of any church, anywhere. If a vision statement applies to every church, it fails to provide unique adaptation, which is essential for survival.

If a vision statement applies to every church, it fails to provide unique adaptation, which is essential for survival.

From Darwin's own words, "There is no fact in the history of the world that is so startling as the wide and repeated extinction of its inhabitants" (Immanuel Velikovsky, *Earth In Upheaval*, p. 43). Natural selection says that, in a harsh climate, the ability to adapt to the natural environment determines who will live and who will die. In today's world, the church finds itself in a drastically changed environment. In the span of fifty years, churchgoers no longer are the majority; persons proclaim themselves spiritual but not religious, and even believers in God do not see the church as a place with sustenance or authority for the spiritual quest. As during the first three centuries of Christianity, Christians find themselves in a harsh climate. Local churches can learn from the adaptive abilities evidenced in nature. Let's take a look at how some fish have joined the finches and mice in adapting to thrive.

Consider the stickleback fish that live in the Pacific Ocean. The stickles on their bodies have a purpose—they make the fish difficult to swallow. Stickles are a vital asset for this species to survive in an ocean filled with predators. There was a population of stickleback fish found in a lake, cut off from the ocean. Over the years of life in the lake, an adaptation (mutation) happened. The stickles disappeared from the fish who lived in the lake. Since there were no Pacific Ocean predators in the lake, the stickles were no longer necessary.

Some local churches still have outdated stickles, which make them hard to swallow. A stickle could be adult classes led by a talking head with no discussion time. Another might be robes worn in worship, or anthems sung in Latin, or rooms designated off-limits to coffee and refreshments, or having visitors stand up in worship and identify themselves. Stickles are the barriers we erect to limit our in-

34

teraction with our neighbors or cause them not to darken our doors! If a stickle is no longer helpful in making new disciples for the transformation of the world, then mutate into life without stickles! Both the Arizona mice and the stickleback fish have been able to thrive since adapting to their new environments. Congregations likewise need to adapt to thrive in their unique environmental settings.

Church cultures adapt through open debate and sometimes outright battles! The battle between Peter and Paul was epic. Peter wanted Paul to do things as the believers did in Jerusalem. Paul, on the other hand, believed that the local church culture of early Christians must adapt if new disciples were to be made in the world outside of Jerusalem. We can catch verses reflecting this mighty debate throughout the New Testament:

> Understand that in the same way that Abraham *believed God and it was credited to him as righteousness*, those who believe are the children of Abraham. But, when it saw ahead of time that God would make the Gentiles righteous on the basis of faith, scripture preached the gospel in advance to Abraham: *All the Gentiles will be blessed in you.* Therefore, those who believe are blessed together with Abraham who believed. (Galatians 3:6-9)

Paul confirms the adaptation of new disciples in the Gentile world, away from the early church culture of Jerusalem to this new culture of Christians, with these verses from that same chapter:

> You are all God's children through faith in Christ Jesus. All of you who were baptized into Christ have clothed yourselves with Christ. There is neither Jew nor Greek; there is neither slave nor free; nor is there male and female, for you are all one in Christ Jesus. Now if you belong to Christ, then indeed you are Abraham's descendants, heirs according to the promise. (vv. 26-29)

Paul knew his purpose was to make new disciples of Jesus for the transformation of the world and he demonstrated that he would do whatever it took to achieve this purpose. He did not refuse to eat food offered to idols, and he named the "unknown God" of Mars Hill as Jesus Christ (Acts 17:23). He never shied away from open debate with synagogue leaders or ruling elders. He did not try to play nice, gloss over their differences, or placate his supporters.

Local churches find themselves in unique ministry settings. Just like the Jerusalem believers were adapted to a Jewish Christian setting, Gentile Christians were adapting to a world dominated by the gods of Mars Hill. The different cultures are not good or bad; they are just different. The Jerusalem Christianity would not have survived in a Gentile world. To carry the gospel beyond a small circle of believers, they had leaders with both the capability and the freedom to make ongoing adaptations to new environments.

The Need for Leaders

It sounds so simple and straightforward, yet time and again, wonderful ideas fail to have the desired impact. This is because the work of adaptation will not just happen. Our churches must be led in these changes by leaders with certain characteristics uniquely needed in the church today. Some of these characteristics are the same as those needed in the first century, like the need for prophets, evangelists, and apostles. Some of the characteristics are adaptations to today's church culture, like the need to remain nonanxious. Because the purpose of North American churches has become so diffuse and confused, leaders today must be clear, bold communicators with the skills to keep large groups of people on track.

There is evidence that we are ill-equipped, poorly trained, anxious, and rudderless as leaders in the local church today. There are not enough adaptive leaders, clergy or lay, in our local churches. Adaptive leaders think on their feet and respond creatively to the unique environment where they live and work. Adaptive leaders are courageous risk takers. Therefore, when an environment presents a unique challenge to the organism's survival, the effective leader will adapt by whatever means are necessary to ensure that survival. These leaders are nonanxious and well aligned with their purpose of making new disciples of Jesus Christ for the transformation of the world.

Adaptive leaders think on their feet and respond creatively to the unique environment where they live and work.

Adaptive leadership is not the only quality in short supply in our local churches. From Dr. Kim Cape, General Secretary of the Board of Higher Education and Ministry of The United Methodist Church, "The local church does not have enough prophets, apostles, and evangelists" (personal conversation with Karen [author]). She is referring to Ephesians 4, where Paul writes about how the local church might structure its common life together: "He gave some apostles, some prophets, some evangelists, and some pastors and teachers. His purpose was to equip God's people for the work of serving and building up the body of Christ until we all reach the unity of faith and knowledge of God's Son" (vv. 11-13).

We are overloaded in the church with pastors and teachers. We cannot survive with clergy and lay leaders who are predominantly pastors and teachers, even though these pastors and teachers may be extraordinarily gifted, "mature adults... fully grown, measured by the standard of the fullness of Christ" (Ephesians 4:13). These pastors and teachers do not fill all the needs for healthy, vibrant, and passionate church life. Nearly all leaders, lay and clergy alike, are trained to practice the gifts of pastoring and teaching *at the expense* of being apostles, prophets, and evangelists.

Pastors care for the people. That work is important and never ending. There are persons in crisis or emotional distress all around us who can grow if they have partners to walk with them through the stress that they experience. If we are caring Christians, then we will have persons in our Christian community who are available to meet the demands of the needy. Teachers are critical. Intentional faith development for parishioners is essential if anyone is to grow in their faith. By and large, both pastors and lay leaders of our local churches have been trained in pastoral/congregational care, as well as being gifted teachers in the church. What has been neglected is our training to be apostles, prophets, and evangelists. One pastor I heard from said, "I signed up to be a pastor and now they want me to be a leader. No one trained me to do that!"

Apostles, prophets, and evangelists do leadership work in reaching beyond the church's walls to unchurched people. Today's church needs our pastors and lay leaders to adapt from a purpose that limits itself to the functions of caregiving and teaching alone (as noble and important as these tasks are) into the broad-based functions of leadership that include apostles, prophets, and evangelists.

Even our seminaries have abdicated their responsibility to train our local church pastors to be evangelists. At a well-respected seminary, one entire day of a board meeting with faculty was set aside to ask the question: "What are we doing well, and what do we need to improve upon?" Compliments far outnumbered complaints. The seminary faculty was filled with brilliant minds and committed teachers. Toward the end of the day, one board member challenged the faculty members in attendance:

"I would like to hear an answer to the following question from each one of the faculty members. 'How does your core discipline, the subject area that you teach, train pastors to make new disciples of Jesus for the transformation of the world?'"

Surprisingly, no faculty member could answer the question. One faculty member suggested that his area of study had no connection to making new disciples of Jesus for transformation of the world. One other faculty member actually took offense that such a question was asked in the first place.

"We are a diverse faculty. It would be impossible to impose such expectations on our faculty members. We are not even of one voice in understanding that 'equipping students to make disciples of Jesus for the transformation of the world' is our job," she said.

It is not only our local churches that have forgotten who they belong to. Like our local churches, some of our seminaries have also failed to adapt to the church's new needs and environment. In short, too many mainline seminaries are simply not teaching prospective pastors how to fulfill our overarching purpose, to make disciples of Jesus for the transformation of the world. Our seminaries have dropped the ball.

According to a leadership survey reported on by Helen Lee in *Leadership Journal* titled "Missional Shift or Drift?" (*Christianity Today Online*, Nov. 7, 2008), pastors not only have sensed the drift in our churches over the last few decades but also feel a shift happening in their own thinking and identified five areas where the shift had occurred in their own focus as pastor:

1. Affirming the whole gospel

2. Not looking to a megachurch model

3. Focusing on making disciples

4. Encouraging a missional mind-set as a means of spiritual formation

5. Establishing partnerships to advance the gospel

The report also observed the following:

> Perhaps the greatest challenge for today's pastors comes in the form of a congregation that does not understand or support the leader's changing perspective. The Leadership survey discovered that many pastors see a gap between their understanding of the gospel and church's mission and the congregation's view of the gospel and mission. (Lee, "Missional Shift or Drift?")

Leaders not only need to be ahead of their congregations on these matters, but they must be prepared to lead adaptive changes. To do that, church leaders must learn to manage their own anxiety.

From Anxious to Adaptive Leaders

As the congregation hears the call for adaptation inside the local church, you can count on a corresponding rise in congregational anxiety. Adaptation brings changes, and change, even welcome, necessary, happy change, is disruptive and disconcerting to those involved. Nonadaptive leaders are anxious leaders. Don't forget that leaders who have been lifted to leadership positions under an alternative purpose will not be pleased to transition from what they know and find comfortable into this new species of Jesus followers. Long-term leaders who cannot or will not adapt have incentives to continue behaviors that contribute to stagnation and decline. The incentives are outlined in our last book, *Ten Temptations of Church: Why Churches Decline and What to Do about It* (Abingdon Press 2012).

Nonadaptive leaders are anxious leaders.

Adaptive leaders will encounter resistance. What does adaptive leadership look like? Specific adaptive actions are difficult to list, because adaptivity by its nature is specific to different situations. Consider, though, the following conversation, which could be heard in any church. Listen to the nonadaptive, long-term leader who does her best to keep things as they have always been.

> For the first time in decades, I will not be at our (governing board) meeting. I appear not to be on anything, so I will not be needed. I do feel that since I have been a leader for more than five years, I could have been personally told—but I guess not. Apparently, people are not as important as the current agenda.

Now, hear a healthy, mature response from an adaptive leader:

> A ball was dropped here, which I regret. However, you are needed in all of your positions through the end of this year (governing body, personnel committee, and the worship team). More important, in 2013 you will have more time and energy for the ministries you will be involved in with women, worship/media, and as spiritual formation

team member. You are needed! We are overdue for leader-ship turnover. Too many of us have held on to our positions for too long. Our new process brought forward many new names for leadership, so the leadership team was able to dis-cern ways to spread the responsibilities and bring in new faces, several of those being younger, such as Carol Smith as governing board chair and Donald Brown [fictitious names] as lay leader. Folks like you and me are the current back-bone, but folks like Carol and Donald are the future of our local church. I believe leaders who have held positions of leadership for a long time such as you, me, and many oth-ers are called now to support the calling of new leaders into ministry. Your presence and blessing of the election of this new leadership team is important. Come tonight. It is not on the agenda but trust me, the current leadership will be acknowledged and thanked. Help us move forward.

Regrettably, few of our current local church leaders practice adaptive skills; therefore, few of our leaders are capable of such a healthy, deeply discipled, mature response as the one modeled here. Notice that the outgoing church lay leader complains that these new adaptations of finding new leadership lack basic care for people, as evidenced by the comment, "Apparently, people are not as important as our current agenda."

Beware of invitations to feel guilty and complaints that ques-tion the adaptive leader's sensitivity to others. If we capitulate to the old, nonadaptive ways, then we will fawn over every church friend or member who feels neglected and unloved. The future of our local churches will be held hostage by nonadaptive leaders who believe the church exists to meet their own personal needs rather than to make new disciples of Jesus for the transformation of the world.

Beware of invitations to feel guilty.

Edwin Friedman explains that we are prone to give in to these high-maintenance, needy, nonadaptive church folks because we want to keep the peace. We are tempted to hear the cries of the unhealthy voices and placate them in the name of good pastoral or congregational care. There must be a way to insist on rotation of local church leadership and also proclaim to those rotating off, "Well done, good and faithful servant." The bottom line is, *nonadaptive church members must not have the power to distract us from reclaiming our true identity and purpose.*

Leaders Use the Power of Alignment

John had lunch with the organizer of a statewide cause, a great guy who was deeply committed. Since the organizer knew John was sympathetic with this cause, over lunch he asked if the church would make a donation to the organization. The conversation went something like this:

> "We are a struggling organization," he began. "Our budget is nonexistent. We need money for the cause. Would your church be willing to make a donation?"
>
> "How will monetary contributions help you fulfill your purpose?" John asked.
>
> "We would be able to finance a rally and bring in a nationally known speaker," he replied, somewhat confused by the question. "We would be able to hire a very part-time volunteer recruiter."

John pressed forward.

> "But what will help you fulfill your purpose?"
>
> "I don't understand what you are asking. Tell me more," he answered, indicating an openness to hear from a new voice.
>
> "I see your purpose written as a vision statement on your pamphlet," John responded. "It seems to me that you are very successful in preaching to the choir. At small conventions people tell compelling personal stories about why your cause needs to succeed, small public demonstrations

take place on behalf of the cause and each year legislation with no hope of passage is introduced to further your cause. Remember that definition of insanity, doing the same thing and expecting different results? The problem is what will you do with the money you want from the churches to help you accomplish your purpose? These activities are noble and valuable things to do, but how are they achieving your purpose? Every organism is limited in how many things it can do. Each organism must do only the things that fulfill its purpose," John offered.

Each organism must do only the things that fulfill its purpose.

"I think I understand what you are saying," he said. "What if we presented a bill that may have a decent chance of passage?" (Here he proposed a specific plan of action in the form of legislation that would at least be a first step in furthering their cause.)

"Now you're talking!" John replied, hoping his friend would hear the encouragement.

"This would allow us to measure the impact such a first step would have on the problem," he continued. "And, if the statistics here report out like in all other parts of the country, we will have hard data to show that our goals and proposals are workable and accomplish an overall societal good."

"And you will be further down the path of fulfillment of your purpose, and your supporters will have new clarity about the group's self-definition," John replied.

For many good and worthy causes, such as prison reform; education reforms; or advocacy around issues of poverty, violence, and so on, conventions are held, speakers are heard, and hand-painted cardboard signs shout each groups' position. These actions may be ways of encouraging the passionate to keep the faith and push on. But when such activities continue unabated year after year, **the understanding of purpose begins to shift into alignment with the activities**. This is because we feel most encouraged when we see results. Organizing a rally for the faithful is much easier than achieving significant public change, just as having a dinner for all the church's regular members and attenders is easier than planning an event that will reach people beyond your walls.

This is one example of alignment. We need to align our behaviors to our purpose. Behaviors outside our purpose may be good and worthy, but if they do not help us fulfill our purpose, then they weaken the organism overall and create confusion for the organization members.

For all the activities you or your church support, are you any closer to achieving your real purpose or goals than you were the year before? If not, then it's time to reexamine your methods. Why, when you keep doing the same thing over and over, do you expect different results?

The environment has changed, but the church continues to pretend that everything has stayed the same. Maybe we know deep down that our environment has changed forever, but we cannot, for the life of us, envision the necessary adaptations we, the church, must make to thrive in the new environment. We are not only out of alignment with our purpose as Christians, but we are failing to thrive because too much of our energy, financing, and leadership are lined up behind the purposes of fellowship, nurture, and even inwardly focused study. Most churches can get more people to sign up for a study on what the Bible says about the purpose of the church than to actually get out and embody the purpose of the church in their own lives.

Adapting to a new environment takes time, of course. Evolutionary changes can take generations and even centuries, but the world of finches can adapt to a rapidly changing environment fairly quickly in order to fulfill their purpose.

We have hummingbird feeders out our back door and love watching hummingbirds land and drink down the nectar (they have adapted!). One day, one of the guards fell from one of the four small feeding tubes and got swept up in the leaves after a massive cleanup. The guard is to prevent any bird without the hummingbird's distinctive beak from drinking up the nectar. It took one baby finch only a few hours to find the unguarded tube. When the finch first started coming to the hummingbird feeder, it was no bigger than the hummingbirds themselves. We could only tell them apart by the too-long-stillness of the wings and the absence of the extended beak. We were fascinated as we watched the tiny bird go to the feeder again and again. As long as the finch was about the size of the hummingbirds, they tolerated it at the feeder. But after a few days, the whole finch family had been brought in on the new food source, and the baby, growing quickly from feeding on the easy, rich diet, was soon full-size and able to run off any hummingbird who wished to light. At that point, we realized we had left the guard off too long, and we quickly found a replacement, making it impossible for any of the finches to feed there any longer.

To our surprise, the original finder of the new food source continued to come to the feeder several times a day. The finch would perch at the stand and try to feed, hopping in turn to all four tubes. It would repeat this several times, and finally perch on top of the feeder as if claiming it for its own, even though it was no longer a food source. We thought the finch's behavior would last a day or two, three at the most, but for almost three weeks, the finch continued to check the hummingbird feeder as a food source. Eventually, the interloper visited less frequently, and finally its experiment with adaptation seemed to end, and with that, the hummingbirds gradually returned to the feeder.

The activity of feeding off the nectar aligned perfectly with the finch's purpose: to eat and grow. When the activity no longer enabled the finch to achieve its purpose, the behavior continued for a while, maybe longer than expected, but eventually the behavior no longer aligned with the finch's purpose of eating to survive, and the finch abandoned the feeder altogether.

Such examples of adaptations demand that we remember the following three things:

45

1. Remember who you belong to (identity).

2. Keep your purpose in front of you.

3. Align every behavior with your purpose.

If the purpose of a business is to make as much money as possible, that business must choose behaviors that align with making a profit. Decisions must be made based on what resources are available to achieve that purpose. If the business has ten phones and ten employees to work the phones, then it is possible that making cold calls to prospects might be the best choice for achieving the purpose of making a profit.

The business might have made some adaptations through marketing. If resources are available for the Internet and marketing by mail, then perhaps cold calls will no longer be the best use of time, since prospects have identified interest in the product with a return envelope or a message on the company's website. *Alignment* means to adapt and use resources for the strongest path to fulfill your purpose.

Still wondering? How about a sports metaphor? The baseball team that is built with speed and quick hands in the field foremost in mind is not likely to hit many home runs. Yet the purpose is to win the game. A small shortstop who gets to the plate and swings for the fences is not using his resources to the best advantage in fulfilling his team's purpose, to win the game. The small shortstop should try to hit the ball in the gaps or draw a walk. Adapt to the resources available; if necessary, cut down your swing, become a singles hitter, and get into alignment with the team's purpose.

The application for local churches is clear. We need to recognize the uniqueness of our local church environment. We need to know who we are trying to reach and what kinds of transformational doors God is opening for us. We need to adapt our leadership and resources to our current setting and align our leadership, finances, and members behind this vision.

Not All Churches Are Alike

Whippets are a crossbred dog, half small greyhound and half terrier. The greyhound is a fast breed, while the terrier is a hunter. English hunting enthusiasts recognized that the greyhound was faster than the prey they wished to hunt but the greyhound would not chase the game. Likewise, they knew the terrier was a fierce hunter but not fast enough to catch the desired prey. The cross-breeding of these two breeds was an intentional adaptation to fulfill a specific purpose. Alignment was achieved. Small greyhounds were bred to terriers and novelty was born, the whippet. The whippet became successful in hunting rabbits and other small game in the English countryside.

When we began our positions in new-church development, we were each sent to a New Church Development convocation in Houston, Texas. John attended in 1980, and Karen in 1984. We were more than receptive to this opportunity for learning. At each convocation, the first presenter was a youthful pastor who explained that his new church was launched on the first Sunday in Advent. The first worship service attendance count was 526, and by the time Karen took the training, the new Houston congregation had built an impressive sanctuary to seat their still-growing congregation. Houston would eventually be home to several mega congregations; the growth in housing, jobs, schools, and new residents in the area was record setting.

At John's new church, they had already had the first worship service when he arrived, in the church's infancy, almost sixty people were regular in their worship attendance. They even had an average of one new family visiting each week. At Karen's church, there were more than one hundred in attendance, but rapid neighborhood development was still years away.

All new church development projects are different. Each local church, whether new, 150 years old, or somewhere in between, is unique. The new churches we served in Austin were unlike the new churches in the Houston area. The model we were given was good. But it had to be adapted to Austin's very different environment. If we

47

expected to be fed by rapidly growing suburbs, our churches would not survive.

All local churches exist in particular settings for ministry. Each local church is a different adventure. We do what we can, with what we have, where we find ourselves. Neither of us was in Houston with an average attendance in worship of 526, in a high school gym where all of the local families would know of our start-up. Our churches' neighborhoods did not have two of the largest homebuilders in the United States finishing fifteen new homes every day. We did not have twelve to fifteen new first-time visiting families in worship every week! John was worshiping in a country-and-western dance hall, on the perimeter of an area that had not yet experienced significant growth. Karen's church had hastily put up a metal building since no meeting place was available.

After a number of years we moved to a one-hundred-plus-year-old center-city mother church that had been in decline for fifty years. On the first Sunday we asked a staff member, "How many first-time visiting households have attended this church over the past three months?" His answer? "None." Not one. Was this a church that had not paid any attention to first-time visitors for decades or a church that had essentially become invisible to its community?

The next church we served was a church that fifty years before had moved from an urban center five miles to the north. The planners had been forward thinking. They assumed rightly that the population growth would move north, away from the old downtown. Yet when the neighborhood to the west of their new location experienced significant decline in housing values, they were unable to adapt to their new neighbors. "How many members of this church live west of our location?" "Maybe a couple, I can't think of any names though," was the answer. They turned their face to the east, where the money and commerce had settled. They seemed unaware of the people who lived in their own neighborhood unaware of the problems those residents faced and the dreams they held.

Adaptation is never finished, but to adapt to the congregation's unique location and environment is a strong beginning. Without some internal adaptations, which we call cultural adaptations, the environmental adaptations that we make will not give us our best chance to survive and thrive. True adaptation requires more than simply changing color or eliminating a stickleback barrier over the years. The external adaptations we make to our surrounding environment will come to naught if the culture inside our local churches hasn't changed. Recall the sampling of reasons why the unchurched do not consider organized churches as sources of spiritual nourishment and expression: too political, hypocritical, judgmental, not concerned with social justice, exclusive, and so on. All these labels are rooted in the perceived or real behavior of church members. The extent to which the labels are rooted in real behavior will make the difference between the adaptation taking hold or it becoming just another fad or program that "we tried that didn't work."

The external adaptations we make to our surrounding environment will come to naught if the culture inside our local churches hasn't changed.

We will never just fall into adaptive change; we must choose to go there. Intentionality is a necessary step in the adaptive process. We must identify who we want to be, what we want to do, and as adaptive leaders, take decisive steps to fulfill our purpose. Be intentional and avoid a shotgun approach or trying something just because it worked in another church somewhere. Adapt to where you are.

We can make the necessary adaptations that will not only fight off possible extinction, but will carry us to a place where local churches can thrive. Following examples from the animal world, we can make necessary adaptations, or mutations, to accomplish our goals. While retaining our original purpose as followers of Christ, churches can intentionally adapt to whatever we need to be in order to accomplish God's dream in our location for ministry.

The chart below helps illustrate just some of the environmental adaptations each church needs to make. Along with identifying new, nonanxious leaders and implementing the practice of alignment, we can remove barriers, change our reputation in the community, discover our community's unique demographics, engage our gifts, and thus open doors for new life.

Environmental Adaptations How relevant is the church to its environment?	Cultural Adaptations How open is the church to being relevant?
Age / employment of area residents	Scarcity to abundance
Church interest and/or preference of area residents	Entitlement to egalitarianism
Ethnicity, gender, and sexual orientation and marital status of area residents	Somber to playful
Socioeconomic demographics of area residents	Limited access to trust
Degree of diversity present	Ignoring to embracing neighbors
Rural, suburbs, or urban	Predictability to freedom
Established or transient population	Marginal members to deep disciples
Nearby business, schools, and community resources	Baby steps to giant leaps
Types and skills of leaders inside and outside the congregation	Suspicion to grace
Community issues and concerns of area	Generic to self-defined

Part Three

Ten Cultural Adaptations for the Church

The following ten adaptations tell the story of calling our congregations into a viable and exciting future. In order to adapt, a congregation must begin an intentional process of moving from one thing to another. The congregation must recognize what is holding them back. Attitudes like scarcity, entitlement, somber life, limited access, and malice all seep into the culture of a congregation. They become part of the church's DNA. Attitudes and behaviors such as ignoring the neighborhood around them, predictability, inviting marginal membership, seeing baby steps as big change, and generic church behaviors keep a church rooted in the past. Congregations must adapt to a culture of abundance, egalitarianism, play, trust, embracing of the neighborhood and location, freedom, deep discipleship, taking giant leaps, owning mistakes, and self-definition. You may already be at work on some of these adaptations, and if so, celebrate! The others will come as your congregation has the foresight and courage to bring them into existence.

In order to adapt, a congregation must begin an intentional process of moving from one thing to another.

---

1. From scarcity to abundance

2. From entitlement to egalitarianism

53

3. From somberness to playfulness

4. From limited access to trust

5. From ignoring the neighbors to embracing the neighbors

6. From predictability to freedom

7. From marginal members to deep disciples

8. From baby steps to giant leaps

9. From suspicion to grace

10. From a generic culture to a self-defined culture

Adaptation #1—From Scarcity to Abundance

Some congregations always focus on what they do not have. A church can believe they are stuck and have no options. They can feel victimized by neighborhood changes, loss of members, and poor leadership. These dark clouds emerge in the language of scarcity. There simply isn't enough: time, money, volunteers, leaders, opportunities. Scarcity has become the standard excuse. Church leaders have historically believed the following:

"If we just had a really good preacher, our congregation would grow."

"If we just had more young people, we would grow."

"If we just had a pastor who would visit more, we would grow."

"If we just had a great Sunday school program, a stronger choir, more members to share the financial burden, and covered dish dinners for fellowship, we would be a stronger local church."

In a community in South Tucson, Arizona, a part-time pastor took leadership of a small congregation. This new pastor was not a young man, but he was filled with passion and energy. The members of that congregation suffered from a low-grade depression, that is, they believed their resources were scarce and that their abilities to pursue ministry were limited. Here is what they said:

"Our congregation is so small, we cannot really do anything."

"Our people are on fixed incomes, so our budget will always be small."

"Our congregation is limited in what we can do because all of our members are older."

At this church there had been pastors rotating through every one to two years. The last pastor moaned, "I keep preaching and teaching about what is possible here, but the people say they are too tired and too old to do anything."

There was no hope to be found, and yet this new pastor saw things a different way. He followed a simple rule: Create the vision, share the vision with the people, and then establish "buy-in" while bringing them along. Early on, he was challenging the congregation to adapt to a new culture of abundance while moving away from the culture of scarcity.

- The church was located in a poor neighborhood, but it was sitting on more than five acres of land.
- The neighborhood watch group needed a place to meet, so the church not only offered its facility but also recruited a few congregants to attend every meeting.
- The mobile clinic needed a once-a-week location for seeing uninsured and underinsured persons, so the church offered its parking lot and set up a hospitality station inside the clinic's makeshift waiting room.
- Children needed something to do during the summer, so a mobile sidewalk Sunday school was brought on-site along with a new community-advertised vacation Bible school.
- A food pantry was established onsite.

- A charter school specializing in the arts built a building onsite, replacing a preschool program that was openly hostile to the local church.
- The pastor wore a clerical collar, which provided a bridge for the predominantly Latino neighborhood population.
- The pastor walked the neighborhood every day, saying "hello" to persons near the church, hearing their stories, and sharing the local church story.

After these remarkable adaptations, the congregation members said to the pastor, "You know, we are much younger now than when you came."

It is not about expanding the program of this or any other local church. This church had adult Sunday school, covered-dish dinners, building and grounds work days, and an all-church garage sale as well as worship every week. It is not that they were under programmed. Congregation members and leaders in the local church know how to keep busy, but we are often busy with activities that fail to achieve our purpose. We keep busy and rarely pause to consider how our activities lead our local church to health and vitality. Doing more stuff is not the pathway to bringing about desired health in local churches. We need to adapt to a new way of seeing our environment and resources.

As the congregation grew, people who only spoke Spanish came to worship. On rare occasions, church participants who did not speak English came to the English-speaking pastor for counseling. One might think the language barrier would be too difficult to overcome, but this pastor found a way to communicate caring and compassion.

There was no infusion of capital, yet the congregation was living a new, adapted life of abundance. In this congregation, we see clearly an emerging, adaptive culture of abundance toward building and people resources.

There was no infusion of capital, yet the congregation was living a new, adapted life of abundance.

For those who are mired in the theology of scarcity, there is never enough money. There are never enough pledges to the budget. Evangelistic efforts are spurred forward in hopes that new members will come on board to spread the financial burden around. One local church business manager, upon hearing of six new members joining the church that Sunday, asked without apology, "How many of them are PUs?"

"What do you mean by *PUs?*" asked the confused pastor.

"Paying units," the business manager said. "How many are paying units?"

As I am sure most of us have heard many times, it is more difficult for folks to talk about money than it is for them to talk about sex. But this is not necessarily true. Churches are more than willing to talk about having very little or no money. Leaders in our churches speak of their congregation's financial limitations ad nauseam. Take a look at the following letter sent out by a local church financial coordinator to members and friends of the church:

Dear Church Members and Friends,

I hope you have felt the renewed energy level at church as I have. Aren't the music and colorful banners great? We are on the home stretch in the financial campaign for our budget. Just so we have an idea of what you may be giving to the church during the coming year, would you mind filling out the enclosed card? Our minister, Fred, is asking for extravagant generosity, but feel free to give anything you are comfortable with. Furthermore, this card is just an estimate for our purposes of budgeting. If it turns out that you actually give more or less, that is fine. Even if you cannot commit to anything at this time, please fill out the card and send it in the stamped envelope we have enclosed so we will not bother you with a phone call in January. Blessings as you continue on your spiritual journey,

—Financial Coordinator

This is more a letter of apology than it is an invitation to share the abundant material blessings bestowed on us by God. The letter seems to say, "Just give what you are comfortable giving and please do not feel the need to go beyond that. Please, at a minimum, send the card back with nothing on it so we will not have to bother you with a phone call that will make us both uncomfortable." This letter is a friend to the miser, the glass-is-half-empty member, the "we are older and on fixed incomes" voices, and the theology-of-scarcity leaders. It should have been bathed in the adaptive behavior of abundance.

In that same church, the pastor discovered a budget line item labeled "church maintenance and renovation." There was $89,000 in that designated line item.

> "What is this $89,000 for?" the experienced pastor asked, knowing congregations of scarcity are infamous for socking away money.
>
> "That is for church maintenance and renovation," came the financial officer's answer.
>
> "How much of this money have we used from this line item over the past five years?" the pastor probed further.
>
> "We replaced some windows! But the rest we are saving for a rainy day," he said.
>
> "I feel moisture," began the new pastor. "No, it feels like rain, possibly a downpour—you indicated that resources are scarce here, but $89,000 for maintenance and renovation in a church our size is abundance!"

At least in this case, the $89,000 was in a designated church account and not a foundation. This fund has at least a fighting chance to be spent on the building in the future.

It was time for the stewardship drive at a local church. As a church, we had not embraced the stewardship concept that teaches the world belongs to God and we are but sojourners on this life's journey. We were not yet ready to embrace the mind-set that we are called to be good stewards of what God has given us. The thinking among congregants seemed to be "what we have belongs to us and we will obediently give God a portion of our household excess."

The stewardship campaign faced a major challenge. We lived in a culture of scarcity. In our local congregation we were circling the wagons, protecting our assets, saving for rainy days, and suggesting that, in these difficult financial times, Jesus might have to get along with less just like everyone else. The local congregation was a composite of this prevailing mind-set within individual church families. Still, we went forward with the campaign slogan "It's not about me."

Laypersons and clergy alike witnessed to the idea that giving is not about us and what we want; it is about God and what God wants. During the six-week campaign the congregation was saturated with various ways to get this message out. Our campaign chair reported that someone had taken offense to this campaign and called the chairperson at home:

> "Hello?" an elderly voice said through the phone. "Is this Margaret, the chair of our stewardship campaign?"
>
> "Yes, this is Margaret," came the reply. "How can I help you?"
>
> "Margaret, I wanted to call and let you know that I find this stewardship campaign offensive," the caller shared. "The campaign is titled 'It's not about me,' and that idea is incorrect."
>
> "We certainly mean no offense," answered Margaret in her most caring and diplomatic voice. "Help me understand how this theme has troubled you."
>
> "It is about me!" the voice of protest declared. "It is about my money. I earned it and I will give it to projects that I deem worthy. I will give it to churches that spend it in the way that I think is best!"
>
> "Oh dear," responded Margaret. "I believe everything we have belongs to God: our heart, mind, soul, and our money. It is not about me as a member, but it is about making new disciples of Jesus for the transformation of the world."

The protester gathered herself at the other end of the line and spoke with a now quiet but firm voice of displeasure: "Please take me off the congregation's mailing list."

Two diverse cultures collided. One culture is propelled by a "me-first," personal-preference understanding while the other culture seeks to live out a special purpose apart from self. Cultural adaptation is hard, painstaking work. It takes time and energy, but unless the church adapts, we will not fully live out our purpose.

Many folks have spoken about this cultural collision. Doug Anderson perhaps says it best. Here is what he shared in a presentation at a local church in Phoenix: "We need to move from a preference-driven church to a purpose-driven church. We need to move from a church that does what I want to a church that does what God wants. We need to move from a church that follows my dreams to a church that follows God's dream."

We need to move from a preference-driven church to a purpose-driven church.

It is not unusual for a congregation to reveal a need for cultural adaptation through the use of money. Local church budget line items are one way we have to measure if a congregation is preference driven or purpose driven. Just as anyone can tell what I believe in by examining my checkbook register and my credit card statements, we can tell the belief practices of any congregation through their monthly budget report.

For those churches fortunate enough (or unfortunate enough?) to have a local church foundation, the operational culture can be identified through the foundation's financial decisions as well. One local church foundation did not consider the liquid and fixed assets of the foundation as belonging to Jesus Christ. The foundation was accountable to 501c3 laws and exercised appropriate fiduciary responsibilities in keeping with those laws. This foundation was accountable to no other body. The assets of this particular foundation were used to grow the corpus, four million, whenever possible.

The fear was not "will Jesus be pleased with how these earnings are spent?" The fear was "spending liquid assets makes us vulnerable in this uncertain economy." The culture of scarcity had swallowed up possibilities of ministry from abundance similar to the way that, as in Joseph's dream recorded in Genesis, the seven lean and ugly cows swallowed up the seven healthy cows.

> The seven healthy cows are seven years, and the seven healthy ears of grain are seven years. It's actually one dream. The seven thin and frail cows, climbing up after them, are seven years. The seven thin ears of grain, scorched by the east wind, are seven years of famine. (Genesis 41:26-27)

Dave Ramsey, well-known financial counselor and Jesus follower, offers financial peace workshops that address the scarcity-to-abundance cultural adaptation. Ramsey presents an adaptive pathway that recognizes the uniqueness of every family's financial situation. The first step of adapting to a new culture of abundance, Ramsey says, is to establish an emergency fund. Save up and set aside three to six months' living expenses for life's emergencies. Just as reported in Genesis, the thin and frail cows and the thin ears of grain are coming, and unless preparations for such emergencies are made, these hard times will take us down.

Mary was living on the margins. Her finances were a mess. She suffered from depression, and she worshiped in a church that was also experiencing depression. Mary signed up in her church along with others to take Ramsey's course on financial peace. Listen to her Christian witness to the culture of abundance at the end of her class: "Mark and I used to fight all the time about money. There was not enough. We cut up our credit cards and changed our spending patterns but still there was not enough. We began building an emergency fund by putting a little away each month." She took a deep breath and continued. "We finally made our goal of saving $4,000."

Then a smile crossed her face. "I started the car to drive to work this morning, and I heard that sound that used to throw me into the pit of despair, a loud knocking noise from my transmission." More animated now, Mary brought it home. "But I refused to let it get me down. I told that transmission, 'You can't hurt me now. I am ready for you! I have an emergency fund!'"

Mary had adapted. She once lived in a culture of scarcity, but now she knows a culture of abundance. As a postscript, Mary's adaptive change was one made by many in that church. If Mary and others like her continue to witness to abundance, then this entire local church has a real chance to move from scarcity to abundance in their lives and in their ministry.

Just as Mary moved from scarcity to abundance for her family and their finances, local churches can examine their assets and produce a stronger financial position by tapping into what has, heretofore, gone unnoticed. One new pastor moving to a church adjacent to a major university saw just such an opportunity in her first week on the job. Walking the mid-sized church campus, the pastor noted a huge university serving forty thousand students on one side while directly behind the church was a parking garage. The five-story parking garage was built by the university and served as pay parking for its students.

On the church campus there was a small, fifty-space parking lot that was in poor condition. Other than some evening programs, choir practice, women's groups, church meetings, and the obvious Sunday morning activity, the church rarely used more than ten spaces in this lot at a time. Often, students would sneak into the lot and park, but church folks were constantly shooing these students away. What church wants to be in the "parking lot police" business while simultaneously creating an antagonistic relationship with the very students it should hope to reach?

The new pastor suggested the local church invest in refurbishing the lot: resurfacing, new lighting, and painting. With buy in from the board of trustees at the church, a "pay to park" meter was installed. The cost for parking was just under the cost to park in the adjacent university garage. With a first-year revenue projection of $25,000, the previously declining congregation's "pay to park" venture will be a major cash cow for years to come. What can a previously dispirited congregation do with an extra $25,000 in their efforts to make new disciples of Jesus Christ for the transformation of the world? Keep this question in front of their planning, and this can be the beginning of leaving scarcity behind in the adaptation to abundance based on resources already available to the local church.

Adaptation #2—From Entitlement to Egalitarianism

A longtime member of the local church called the office with a specific request:

"Pastor," the elderly woman began, "my granddaughter has just given birth to a baby boy. He weighed in at seven and one-half pounds. He was nine and one-quarter inches long! This is my first great-grandchild!"

"Congratulations!" came words of celebration from the pastor. "You must be very proud."

"We sure are," the grateful parishioner continued. "We are planning to have the child baptized in three months and would like for you to do the honors."

"I would be delighted," the pastor said. "But I don't believe I know your granddaughter or her husband. Which service do they attend?"

"Heavens, no," giggled the great-grandmother. "They have lived in Colorado ever since my granddaughter finished college. She and her husband both have great jobs in Denver. They love it there."

"Do they have a church home in Denver?" inquired the pastor.

"No, they aren't really into church right now. They're young, still getting settled. Truth be told, I think her mother talked her into doing the baptism here while they visited our family during spring break."

"I'm not sure it is such a good idea to baptize the baby here if the parents live in Denver," the pastor spoke, treading lightly with his long-term member. "Baptism is not only saying 'God loves you just as you are,' but it is almost always done inside of the community of faith where the child will be raised. There is a promise from the local congregation to raise the child in that particular faith community. Hard to do from 1,500 miles away."

"So you are saying you won't baptize my great-grand-baby?" After hearing the unwelcome news, her tone had clearly changed.

"I'm just saying maybe they should hold off a bit, find a church in their neighborhood, and do the baptism there," the pastor replied. "I would be glad to talk with them about this."

Now here came the entitlement eruption.

"Pastor, I am more than disappointed, I am incensed! My family has belonged to this church for three generations. My children were baptized here and their children were baptized here. My family gave the new choir folders in 1973, and my husband went on a mission trip with the church a few years before he died. We have attended every Christmas and Easter for as long as I can remember. We were considering a pledge for this year, but you can forget about that!"

Some folks live out of an old culture that believes membership has its privileges even though we are all best reminded that the church is the one organization that does not exist for the benefit of its members.

Every pastor has a story of a parishioner who has forgotten that the purpose of our congregations is to make new disciples of Jesus for the transformation of the world. In the opinions of many members, seniority and family name carry weight, and demands for better service from pastors salt and pepper many conversations. Entitlement is a culture that ensures continued decline.

One pastor shares an email from a parishioner who stated her objection to the decision of the local church Board of Trustees, the body responsible for all actual and real property of that local church:

You would think they [Board of Trustees] would want to approach this matter with the greatest of care and consideration! This is especially true as this whole church owes my family for the simple fact of its existence. It was my grandfather who was the generous contractor who waited payment and did what he could, pro bono, plus used his many connections to get as much donated as possible. He also served long and well on both the Board of Trustees and Foundation!

What does any local church owe its members? If membership does not have its privileges, then what is the point? In the church of Jesus Christ, membership has its responsibilities. We must be accountable to our purpose. How are we becoming the hands and feet of Jesus to make new disciples for the transformation of the world?

A choir director had to contend with one member of the chancel choir who was unable to behave herself. She was known, on more than one occasion, to get angry during choir rehearsal and throw her music across the room. The choir voted to wear robes during the season of Lent, the six weeks prior to Easter, and this one member refused to wear a robe. Since the choir sat up on the chancel, or stage area, everyone caught the visual of this defiant choir member who did not wear a robe but wore a scowl on her face instead. The frustrated choir director came to the pastor begging for advice.

"I have tried everything. I don't know what to do with her," he said.

"What have you tried?" the pastor inquired.

"I tried printing out rules of conduct for choir members and handing them out at rehearsal. I gave them to everyone, since I didn't want to single her out in front of the others because it might be embarrassing for her."

"Did she conform to the rules?" the pastor asked.

"No, not for a moment," the choir director answered. "Then I asked her to stay after choir for a few minutes. I listened to her angry complaints. I told her how valuable she is to the choir and what a big contribution she makes to her section. I asked her to please not yell at me or the other choir members during rehearsal."

"How did that work for you?" pushed the pastor.

"Not well," the choir director answered. "Shortly after that she threw her music across the room. I asked her why she exploded in anger like that, and she said 'anger is a good and cathartic thing and I have the courage to show my anger while others shrink from it.'"

"I have a suggestion for you," the pastor replied, "but I am afraid you will not like it."

"Go ahead," the choir director answered. "I'll try anything. I am desperate!"

"Here is what you do," the pastor said, leaning forward and lowering his voice a bit. "Try a conversation like this: 'Peggy, the purpose of our church is to make new disciples of Jesus for the transformation of the world. The purpose of the church is not to keep you happy and satisfy your needs. We hope to grow this choir. We cannot grow choir membership if you continue your pattern of behavior. Some restraint from you is necessary if we are to be seen as Jesus followers.'"

"I tried saying something like that but she shot back, 'Jesus got angry and overthrew the tables of the temple in Jerusalem.'"

"Well, remind her what happened to him! She is not Jesus and we do not live in Jerusalem," the pastor continued. "Try ending your conversation with 'I want you to read over the rules of conduct for the choir and abide by those rules. Find a robe to wear this Sunday and be a part of the group. If you aren't able to abide by these simple guidelines, then I'm going to have to ask you to refrain from participating in the choir until you are ready to conduct yourself within these expectations.'"

The director spoke with alarm in his voice, "You cannot kick somebody out of the church!"

"We have no intention of kicking anyone out of the church," the pastor summarized. "Peggy can come sit in the pews and worship here as long as she likes, but being a choir member is being a leader of worship. Being a choir member is not her birthright as a longtime member. It is not something to which she is entitled. It is a privilege and there is a responsibility to be a team player and behave as a Christian disciple that goes with the privilege."

Much of our difficulty in adapting from a culture of entitlement to a culture of egalitarianism is a result of our being unwilling to restrain bad behavior in longtime members. If dysfunctional people rule the community, then it is impossible to make new disciples of Jesus for the transformation of the world. One of our seminary professors was fond of saying that a problem surfaces when we try to treat crazy makers like normal people. We try to bring order through logic and reason. This does not work with crazy makers. Crazy makers make craziness. That is what they do. It does not work to treat them like they are normal.

We are unwilling to restrain bad behavior in longtime members.

Peggy sounds like a crazy maker to me. Peggy is loved by God, to be sure, but at the least she will keep any small-church group from growing new disciples and, at worst, she will run off some of the followers of Jesus already there. Who needs that kind of drama in their lives? The other choir members will drop off and drop out, seeking another place to sing. Church folks, choir directors, and even pastors must stand their ground against entitlement and bullying. The stakes are too high. We cannot let them eat us up.

The old culture of entitlement, of family nameplates suggesting ownership of sanctuary pews, drive-by baptisms, and tolerating crazy makers needs to end. In its place, we need to grow the culture of egalitarianism where all persons are equal in the sight of God—a culture where no one commands special privilege, a culture where no one has tenure. For many of our local churches, making the shift from entitlement to egalitarianism is a necessary, demanding cultural adaptation.

Adaptation #3—From Somberness to Playfulness

We once served a local church in central Texas. It was an older church that had long been in decline. It was a somber place when we arrived. Every Sunday felt more like a funeral than the joyous worship of God. There was a rigid and unspoken expectation to "do things the right way" permeating the leadership, especially the ushers. The head usher seemed to have tenure, and he ran a tight ship. He was a righteous man, moral and ethical in every way. He was a good man. He was, however, a bit tightly wound. He would stick to the script without fail or deviation. No spontaneity was allowed and extemporaneous behaviors in worship were not tolerated.

One Sunday in worship John messed up. The bulletin clearly said our next worship activity would be the call for offering. John was caught up in the moment and blew right past the offering into the second hymn. (In his defense, we did go back to the offering later on. What mainline Protestant church is going to skip the morning offering altogether?) But at that moment, it was too late to back up; we saw the head usher and all his usher collection-plate peers, standing at the entry of the sanctuary, rudderless and confused. After the hymn, the verbal cues were given to the congregation that allowed us to get back on bulletin track. Hymn sung, offering collected, all was well, or so we thought.

After worship the head usher was primed, and John received a schoolboy dressing-down.

> "John, I can't believe you passed right over the offering. The bulletin clearly says the offering is before the hymn, not after the hymn. Ushers were standing, waiting, confused and unsettled. Did you not see the worship order? You must read the bulletin and follow the prescribed order."
>
> "You have every right to be upset," John answered. "I blew it. I didn't follow the service order, and I apologize. I appreciate your gifts in doing things decently and in order.

You are good at rules. I want to get better at following rules and, with your help, I think I will do better."

"OK," said the usher, a bit disarmed with the warmth and contrition of John's response.

Then, as he turned to walk away, John called out, "Wait, wait, wait, friend. One more thing. You are good at following rules, but you are not so good at play. I am going to learn from you how to follow rules and at the same time, I am going to teach you how to play."

All this was delivered with a big smile and a disarming tone. The usher was taken aback by this new partnership of covenantal transformation, but we are happy to report that he did loosen up before the close of our time together.

The old church culture was often rule based and a bit rigid. Protocol and procedure was often elevated over spontaneity and exuberance. The new culture we seek in adaptation is playful. We know some persons find joy in sticking to the script, but life happens. Interruptions and mistakes show up. We need more than just to go with the flow. We need to play. There is a close correlation between the overall health of a congregation (or an individual, for that matter) and the ability to play. Healthy congregations are more apt to play, while declining congregations find it difficult to play.

Not everyone is a natural at play; some folks need to be taught. Invitations for people to lighten up in church are exploding all around us. At weddings Karen would say to the couple (usually the bride, as most grooms are instructed to show up and hush up),

> "You may want everything to be perfect on your special day, but there is only one guarantee, and that is that something will go wrong. Everything will not proceed according to a tight script. The groom's knees might lock, and he will faint dead away. The flower girl may need an emergency bathroom break. The best man may forget the ring or even the license. The local church sound system may

inadvertently pick up the radio communication from a nearby patrol car. (All of these things have happened in a wedding that one or the other of us have conducted.) The point is, something most likely will go wrong. Try to relax and have fun. Smile, laugh, and enjoy the moment! Perfection is beyond our reach! Twenty years from now, what you will remember most fondly are the unexpected, unscripted moments. Even the mistakes will leave you smiling."

Somber is the ally of perfection. Playful is the pathway to abundant life. We were holding a service in the brand-new sanctuary of a local church located in Austin, Texas. The members and friends of that church waited a long time to worship in their own sanctuary, and their dream was finally a reality. Halfway through John's sermon, the thirty-foot cross suspended from wires behind the altar came loose from the wall and crashed down onto the Communion table. There was an audible gasp from the congregation, as you can imagine, and then an awkward silence.

Somber is the ally of perfection. Playful is the pathway to abundant life.

"Darn," John said, breaking the silence. "I was just getting to the best part!" Most folks released their tension by laughing. "I could go ahead and finish the last two pages of this sermon, but none of you would be listening," he said. "Let's sing a benediction." Karen then added, "Anyone with construction skills, meet us on the chancel after worship!" The event could have been horribly somber and disturbing, but instead, everyone was laughing and in good spirits. At a twenty-five-year anniversary of that church, everyone remembered the event with laughter and smiles.

If you are stuck in a somber culture and want to create a more playful culture, it might help to rename some of the church's traditional program ministry efforts. Play with titles. Why have "vacation Bible school" when we could have "Captain Underpants Meets Jesus!" (or whoever is the kids' current favorite character). Invite kids to wear the costumes of a favorite superhero. Which VBS would your child want to attend? Changing titles is a great way to enter into the world of play. One lay leader recruited church friends and members to share their skills with their local church. No somber, dry, and uninspiring offerings for the fall brochure; he had other ideas. He decided to build an entire small-group ministry around the following catchy titles:

Soccer Players Seeking Goals Here—convened by a local soccer coach.

Parents Learn What Love Really Is Here—convened by the lone young adult couple in the congregation.

Kids Find Out Who the Real Boss Is Here—convened by the Sunday morning nursery attendant.

Guitarists Find a Different Rhythm—led by the contemporary band's guitar player.

PhDs Phind God Here—led by three tenured professors at the college.

Pharmacists Having Phun—led by a pharmacist who worked with persons who are living on the margins.

Other titles kept coming. "Green Means More than Recycling," "Homeless Have Bed and Breakfast Here," "Service Means More than a Smile Here," "Mexico Is More than Spiritual Tourism Here." The local church has to have passionate leaders for these small groups, but the title can go far in your efforts to communicate that this local church is unique and even playful!

Adaptation #4—From Limited Access to Trust

In Austin, Texas, John arrived as the new pastor less than six months into the worship life of a new church. The members had a great time worshiping in a temporary home, a country-and-western dance hall. They had adult Sunday school classes meet under beer signs, carried hymnals and nursery toys in the trucks of their automobiles, and even used club soda for a surprise adult baptism. Each morning they pulled chairs out on the dance floor for worship. Though their dance-hall days were fun, it was great when the time came for them to move into their first multipurpose building.

In the course of conversation, a building committee member asked, "Who should get keys to the new building?"

"How about giving a key to every member family in the church?" one leader suggested.

"Sounds good to me," said one member.

"Sure, why not?" replied another.

And so a new culture was brought into being. Some would say that this new church had already established a new and different culture by adapting to its life in a country-and-western dance hall. The "key for every member" movement in the new facility was not hurt by the fact that on two different Sundays during the last three years, the dance hall was accidentally locked on Sunday morning when it came time to worship. A pickup bed was the chancel area of necessity on those days, and they certainly didn't want to revisit any similar emergencies in the future. Still, the key-for-every-member decision was a cultural adaptation away from all other local churches we know.

This new culture did not sit well with a member of the new church who had joined after they moved into the new facility. He had a difficult time transitioning from his preferred limited-access culture into the more adaptive culture of keys for every member. He was a retired field agent for the Internal Revenue Service. He was very agitated when he came to talk with John.

"John," he said, "who gave authorization for every member of the church to be given keys?"

"We talked about it in the governing board," John answered, not knowing the cause of his agitation. "Why do you ask? Is there a problem?"

"Certainly there is a problem," he insisted. "Everyone should not have keys to the church. It simply isn't done!"

"You are correct. To my knowledge it has never been done before," John replied, "but I agree with our other local church leaders. I think this is exciting! Not only does giving out keys to the church lift the burden of having a trustees' chair or the pastor on call 24/7 to come and open up, but it is a wonderful symbol of both trust and responsibility for everyone who joins this community of faith."

"I hardly think so," the man protested. "Distribute these keys, and our church will be robbed blind."

"This is a new church," John offered. "Maybe it is time to risk operating in a new culture of trust."

The retired IRS agent remained unconvinced. On the first Sunday in the new building, he and his wife were the only church members who did not come forward to receive their keys to the building during the worship service. As a side note, there were no reports of theft or vandalism during the remaining twelve years that we served that congregation. The church grew, and our local locksmith sang the doxology.

In many churches there is a policy of limited access. Limited-access churches not only limit distribution of keys to the building but often overregulate the use of buildings and grounds. Wide-open churches could give keys to every member or have a system where individual local church leaders can check out keys as needed. Limited-access churches may not feel trust in the community in which they are located, or they may simply place a high priority on safety and security. Limited-access churches lock gates, update alarm systems, put bars on windows, and even fences around the property. The fences don't really keep anyone out, but they do communicate a message to the area. Limited-access churches maintain an old culture of mistrust and suspicion, which is easily interpreted as a retreat from the community. We're not saying that locking doors at night is a problem. We all do that. We are saying that establishing a culture of trust among church members includes trusting them with the property itself. We are saying communicating trust to the surrounding community means the church needs to be open and accessible during the day.

Establishing a culture of trust among church members includes trusting them with the property itself.

Trusting churches communicate a willingness to take risks and show trust. Wide-open churches are not naïve. They are wise as serpents and gentle as doves. Wide-open churches adapt to a culture that treats all members with dignity and respect. Wide-open churches have adapted from limited access to trust.

Adaptation #5—From Ignoring the Neighbors to Embracing the Neighbors

Sherry Cothran Woolsey is the pastor of a small church in Nashville. In her *Circuit Rider* article of 2012, she described the neighborhood setting for her congregation:

The neighborhood demographics shifted and the community became increasingly urban; the church sold property to survive as its core congregation began to move away and pass away. Gradually, the church building became an island among urban businesses. An empty lot, [once] owned by the church, became a McDonald's. Behind the church, a sold property became a steel worker's union hall. By 2006, the [area where] the church resided...experienced a severe degree of urban blight, and many of the storefronts were empty. ("A Transforming Light in Urban Blight," p. 23)

This same situation occurs in most every city in the country. Members move away from the neighborhood but continue to commute to church. Meanwhile, the neighborhood itself is on life support. Sherry describes people "who love their church with its rich history and are, at the same time, ignoring their neighborhood rather than embracing that neighborhood. The pathway to survival this church had chosen in the past was to sell property, which was tantamount to amputating limbs" (Woolsey, 2012). Out with amputation and in with adaptation. This organism would not survive without radical adaptation. Indeed, this pastor describes how other congregations, who were once thriving in this same neighborhood, had gone extinct:

> Church of Christ, two blocks down, closed its doors in 2008 and sold its lot [regrouping elsewhere with a] few faithful members.... The Presbyterian church turned into a community theater and office space. The Baptist church [sold its property] to a nondenominational church that revitalized the space. West Nashville United Methodist Church found itself on an island between vastly different socioeconomic groups, ghost churches, and diverse ethnic populations.

What could have been a potentially remarkable opportunity for new ministry for these churches was forcefully dampened by low social capital within these churches, and those who remained in these congregations were overwhelmed by years of trying to survive and maintain tradition in constantly changing conditions.

It was time for this local church to adapt from ignoring the neighborhood to embracing the neighborhood. Partnering with organizations such as a local food bank and a mental health group began the church's transformation. Bible studies in Spanish, children's programs, bilingual worship services, English as a second language courses, computer skills training, and a neighborhood VBS furthered their adapt-to-thrive journey.

In our first book, *Not Just a One Night Stand: Ministry with the Homeless*, we wrote about a downtown congregation that had a poor relationship with its neighbors. The owners and occupants of nearby high rises, office buildings, upscale hotels, downtown businesses, and entertainment venues all struggled with how to deal with the large number of people who were without shelter and made downtown San Antonio their home. A ton of money was spent by businesses and residents on 24-hour security and custodial labor to combat graffiti. Travis Park Church was no different. Graffiti adorned the walls and night watchmen were part of the expense of doing church. Tourism was a significant part of city revenue, and the large homeless population was considered a huge problem. Then homeless people began sleeping on local church property.

"What are we going to do?" a church leader questioned. "This is not safe at all!"

"You're right," agreed the missions leader. "This is not safe and something has to be done."

"Then you agree that we must call the police." The first leader pressed forward, feeling emboldened. "We will lobby law enforcement to step up their patrols, and when they discover someone sleeping on the property, those persons will be chased away."

"Oh, no," answered the second leader. "We can't do that! That's not what I meant at all!"

"But you said yourself it is not safe," the first leader replied, now thoroughly confused.

"For the persons sleeping on our grounds, it is not safe. For the persons who happen to be homeless who are sleeping on our property," the second leader explained. "They are at risk, especially the homeless women."

Sure enough, a neighborhood watch program on the property of Travis Park Church was developed by persons who were temporarily homeless for the protection of others who also happened to be homeless. The church leaders who operated out of the old culture of mistrust and ignoring neighbors watched as church leaders who had adapted to a new culture of embracing neighbors facilitated leaders in the homeless community to create a safe sanctuary around the church.

One of the fascinating side effects of embracing the neighbors was the elimination of all graffiti from the walls around the church building. Tagging and destruction of property stopped. The 24-hour security guard was discontinued. The persons who slept around the building's perimeter were very protective of the church that sought to treat them with dignity and respect. Everything can change when people in a neighborhood believe they are embraced by the church.

Churches who have teenage neighbors post signs that prohibit skateboarding. Churches in desperately poor neighborhoods post signs that say, "We refer all requests for help to local shelters and food pantries." Churches with young children all around them are slow to upgrade antiquated nurseries and post warning signs about bringing food and drink into classrooms. This is ignoring neighbors.

In the new culture, churches with teenage neighbors might build a skateboard ramp for use in supervised activities. In the new culture, churches located in desperately poor neighborhoods might start a food pantry, a job program, and recovery groups. In the new adaptive culture, churches surrounded by children might throw neighborhood birthday parties for kids, maybe start a summer arts camp, and make their entire campus more child friendly. Who are your neighbors? The parable of the Good Samaritan teaches us that our neighbors are the people who travel the same road and take up space next to us.

Who are your neighbors?

One local church stood at the crossroads of outrageous wealth and desperate poverty. One mile to the east and north there were million-dollar homes, boutique shops, and high-end restaurants. One mile to the south and west there were modest apartments and a junior high school where 90 percent of the students were on subsidized meals. One mile to the east and north the population was 85 percent Anglo and retired. One mile to the south and west the population was Latino and working class.

This church had blinders on. The only population they could see lived to the east and north. One long-time member realized something had to be done. He went to the junior high school and talked with his neighborhood school's principal:

> "Hi, my name is Alan. I am a member of a local church not more than one mile from here. I understand you have been principal here for several years. First, let me apologize for not talking with you sooner. Our church has not been a good neighbor to you. Now I hope to rectify that oversight. May I ask what are the most pressing needs of the students at your school?"

> The principal responded, thinking, "Here is one more do-gooder clogging my office. When he hears my answer he will run like a rabbit."

> "Reading. Most of our kids are behind at least one grade level in reading skills. Reading at grade level is basic to education. If you want to be a good neighbor, then teach our children to read."

The principal ended this conversation quickly, thanking the well-intentioned church member for coming to visit, secure in the notion that she would never see him again. To her surprise, she got a call from Alan one month later.

> "I am sorry it has taken me a month, but maybe we can help with the reading skills problem," Alan reported. "I have twenty retired adults who are ready to become one-on-one reading tutors with kids after school. I have a van ready to pick up the kids from school once a week and bring them to the church. Since kids are often hungry when school lets out, we will have a snack ready when they get to the church. We will also have a sack supper for them to take home and share with the rest of their families. We can tutor kids to read for thirty minutes at each session. But we don't want to stop there. Many of our retired adults would love to learn how to speak Spanish. Can we trade teaching kids how to read in English for the students teaching us conversational

Spanish? We thought this might be the best way to develop lasting relationships. What do you think?"

It took some time to work out the details, but imagine the intergenerational, interethnic, cross-socioeconomic friendships that developed when this local church and school began to work together. Inside each one-on-one relationship, each participant was a student for thirty minutes and a teacher for thirty minutes. "I have something I can teach you, and you have something to teach me." They ate together and learned together, all because one church leader refused to ignore his neighborhood any longer.

It's true that local schools will differ in their willingness to interact with churches, but don't take no for an answer. Keep after it and persuade them of your good intentions. Be open to what is really needed—besides money. It will cost you some money to be sure, but that won't change your church's image in the community. Only blood, sweat, and tears can do that.

Your unique setting for ministry will be, in large part, defined by your geographic location. If your church is in a new neighborhood with starter homes for families all around you, work to build the best possible children's program, to make new, young disciples of Jesus to transform the world. If your congregation is located next to a college or university, it would be regrettable to neglect a ministry to students, staff, and faculty.

There was a day when, if you wanted to do a new-church-development project in Florida, you would find the best big band musicians available to perform at Sunday morning worship because that was the era and musical reference of the people you were trying to reach. That's not true anymore. Today's new retirees are baby boomers, whose musical preferences changed musical history. They grew up with TV, evolution, and the moonwalks. Embracing your neighbors is an attitude before it's an action.

Embracing your neighbors is an attitude before it's an action.

In a retirement area, van ministries are important because some retirees no longer drive. In another retirement area my friend sought to embrace his neighborhood by establishing a ROMEO group (Retired Old Men Eating Out). We must adapt to our neighborhood to thrive as a local church. Be a good neighbor. Embrace your neighborhood.

The simplest adaptation to embrace your neighbors is to recognize who God is sending to cross your path. The adaptive church will be on the lookout for their neighbors who have been largely ignored.

In an article from the Alban Institute 2011, "A Place for Everybody: A Church at the Intersection of Faith and Disability," Mark Pinsky's book *Amazing Gifts: Stories of Faith, Disability, and Inclusion* is reviewed. Mark has numerous stories of how declining churches have made the adaptation from ignoring to embracing the people of their neighborhood.

One young mother, Sandy, was excited about a new connection to God she had made in her neighborhood church. She wanted to join. She filled out her membership card. One part of the membership records asks that she name other family members. A son named Walter was listed. The pastors, a husband-and-wife team, were curious because they had never seen Walter in church. When the new member was asked about her son, she explained that Walter had a very low IQ and suffered from autism. She thought Walter's inability to self regulate and practice the most basic boundaries would be too much for the local church to handle, so Walter was left at home with his father. She was afraid her entire family would be rejected if Walter were to attend church.

Walter lived within the shadows of that local church. The pastors seized upon this chance to embrace their neighborhood rather than just ignore their neighbors. Mom was encouraged to bring Walter. Mom took that chance. Soon after that, mom was baptized. After mom was baptized, it was time to baptize Walter. Mark Pinsky explains what happened next:

> A strange process began—the small congregation began to re-shape itself around one person and in doing so it found new life. The Kramer-Mills recognized that Walter had a fear of confined spaces so they decided that he and his sister would be baptized outdoors. For several weeks, the clergy-couple rehearsed with Walter—using an empty

bowl on a camping table in the front yard of a nearby farm. The Baptism came off without a hitch.

More extraordinary and loving things began to happen in this local church....They took specific steps to welcome Walter more fully into their life. The people of the church received training in shared life with special needs persons. They joined a group of other faith communities on a similar journey. Momentum grew....Walter was one of them now and he would definitely be treated with dignity and respect in their house of worship.

Pinsky adds more:

The co-pastors put into practice what they learned. The autism task force evolved into the Special Needs Accessibility Project, [including] other developmental needs beyond autism....Walter reached confirmation age and the congregation adjusted its confirmation practice creating a curriculum and ceremony that allowed him to share his faith by participating in the telling of the creation story (his line was "It is good!"), and then acting out his vows. Now, Walter is seen as an integral part of his congregation.

In this heart-warming story, Mark Pinsky points out that Sandy and Walter are both in the neighborhood of First Reformed Church. That church clearly is adapting from a long-standing practice of ignoring their neighbors to embracing their neighborhood. This church is made up of Jesus followers who know that loving their neighbors goes hand in hand with the personal piety of loving their God. Loving Sandy and Walter maintains alignment with both the local church purpose, to make new disciples of Jesus for the transformation of the world, as well as keeping faith with the following scripture:

Jesus replied, "What is written in the Law? How do you interpret it?"

He responded, "You must love the Lord your God with all your heart, with all your being, with all your strength, and with all your mind, and love your neighbor as yourself."

Jesus said to him, "You have answered correctly. Do this and you will live." (Luke 10:26-28)

Adaptation #6—From Predictability to Freedom

Karen can still remember the warm feeling she had inside when reciting the Apostles' Creed, when she started back to church as an adult. She knew every word of the creed by heart. She felt like an insider, and that's just the point. That's not the world we live in now. Most people do not know any creeds by heart, and they probably don't care to, either. While church folks love the predictability of church, the world keeps changing around them and that produces anxiety and stress. Surprises are unwelcome and it is difficult to adjust to even modest changes. If it is familiar, it rules! So how can the culture of predictability move into the culture of freedom? Adaptation is the key. Small changes will not be adequate to actually change the church's culture. If you want to get people's attention, then:

- Move the chancel furniture around
- Change the doxology or eliminate it entirely
- Take out the back four pews
- Move a long-running Sunday school class to a new room
- Change the expected lineup for lay leaders in worship

Do these sound like big changes or small changes? Look at them again. Are any of these the kind of massive shift to a new culture that it will take for the church to experience a resurgence?

We went to serve an old, revered church in the year 1995. One of the first things we did was to look at the worship bulletins from the month prior to our arrival. We found a copy of a worship bulletin from forty years before. The worship order was exactly the same. Prayers, hymns, positioning of announcements, prelude, postlude—all the same.

Not coincidentally, it was discovered that for sixty years this local church had been in decline. No variance, no adaptation, no change for forty years. As with that old expression, this local church had continued to do things the way they had always done things and expected different results.

Worship is the work of the people. If worship has not adapted in sixty years, then we assume that the people of 1955 are the same as the people of 2015. This makes no sense. We are told by social scientists that young people want their local church to be real, relevant, and relational. The churchgoers of 1955, the greatest generation as identified by Tom Brokaw, responded to "should dos" and "ought tos." The young people of today are nothing like the church goers of 1955. They value freedom and love the latest in technology, social media, language, and fashion. In short, they do not want to be defined by the past.

When we offer nothing but our traditions to a population craving the new, it will be hard to get them in the door, much less keep them. But young people today also value timeless ideas, rituals, and practices; they love to rediscover something old that has been repurposed into something brand-new. In February of 2012, John Bell taught a group of clergy some steps in how song leaders might move from a culture of predictability to freedom in service music. This initiative was driven by adaptation. For congregations who do not like to learn new hymns, use the old familiar hymn tunes with new, more relevant lyrics. For congregations learning new music, teach new tunes this way:

- First verse—listen to the song leader.
- Second verse—listen to the song leader and hum along.
- Third verse—join in and sing.

The message was Darwinian. Take what was familiar yesterday and adapt it to today. If our music never adapted to the twentieth century, then it won't do any good to get around to twentieth-century music in the twenty-first century just because it's more palatable! We've lost whole generations. Everything we do on Sunday morning needs to connect with the people we're trying to reach or we will not be able to make new disciples of Jesus Christ for the transformation of the world.

Everything we do on Sunday morning needs to connect with the people we're trying to reach.

Adapting to freedom in a culture that has previously been dominated by a culture of predictability can be costly. As in all the adaptations we talk about, some folks are just not going to come along into a new culture necessary to thrive. Sometimes it can cause pain in the wallet.

A pastor wanted to communicate the meaning of infant baptism during Sunday morning, so with the parents' permission he adapted the sacrament in worship. He asked the historic questions of faith and put water on the baby's head as instructed by his denomination. But then he took the baby out into the congregation, introducing the baby to three different members. The individual members held the baby in their arms while the pastor talked about the relationship that would build between the congregant and the baby. The pastor said when he addressed the congregants

> "Stephanie, you are now in the arms of Frances. Frances is the Sunday school superintendent for our church. Every week, when you come to Sunday school to learn about Jesus, Frances will be there. She will help you learn the stories of the Bible, make sure you get your snack, and comfort you when you are scared.
>
> "Stephanie, you are now in the arms of Bill. Bill has the gift of play. If you learn a new joke, Bill wants to hear it, and he will likely tell you one of his jokes in return. He sets up the waterslide for the kids every summer, and he likes to see children smile more than any other grown-up here.
>
> "Stephanie, Elizabeth is holding you now. She is a kid, like you. She is in the fourth grade. She will be like your big sister here. Elizabeth knows all the neat places to hide in this

church. She will teach you! She also will hold your hand if you are lost and scared."

At the conclusion of the introductions, the pastor took Stephanie back to the front and, before giving her back into the arms of her parents, he said:

"I am giving you back to your parents now, but I want you to remember, you do not belong to them, you belong to God. Sure, they will always be your parents and will provide for you until you are eighteen and go out on your own, or maybe twenty-one, or in today's world, twenty-seven [chuckles all around], but you don't belong to them. You are a child of God and belong to God."

It was unpredictable. It was an adaptation of freedom, honoring the historic tradition of the church while engrafting that child to her new community of faith. One person so loved predictability in her church home that she was angry with the freedom the pastor had exercised in the baptism of Stephanie. The disgruntled member wrote a letter:

This local congregation is no longer to me the church to which I pledged in the [recent finance campaign]. Therefore, I will have to search long and hard to decide if I will honor the balance of my pledge. This has nothing to do with the economy. The day when I go to church and witness a baptism that is sacred rather than a segment from *Saturday Night Live* complete with shills, will be the day I can make that decision. However, as things stand under the current leadership, you better plan your budget without my commitment.

The member who wrote that letter gave a sizable amount to the church budget every year. Here was not-so-subtle pressure to back off adapting to freedom and to bring back predictability. Adapting to a new culture of freedom will mean those who hold predictability sacred will not be happy, yet without adapting to a new culture of freedom, our congregations have no chance to thrive.

In the same church near a university that finally recognized its parking lot as an asset, another asset was recognized. There were twelve to fifteen students each year who received special parking at the church in return for weekly volunteer work. The church office put these students to work filing, folding bulletins, answering the phones, dusting, and cleaning.

These are predictable local church volunteer duties. But these church leaders were adapting away from predictability all the way to creative models of freedom. One student was asked to use his two-hour-per-week volunteer stint to be a webmaster for the church. Two other students agreed to be Sunday school teachers for the children. Two more began playing in the band at the contemporary service. One became the leader of a new group organized for college-age folks. Two more came to worship for one of their hours and stayed to participate in this college-age small group after worship. What do you think will have more power in making new disciples of Jesus among college-age students? Volunteers in the old, predictable jobs, or volunteers in these new, creative jobs?

In adaptation to freedom we update our thinking. We take risks. We have to try new things, even when we are apprehensive about leaving the comfort of what has become our predictable way of doing things. In other words, we have to adapt to what is happening now.

A couple of years ago, while on vacation with a car full of other baby boomers, we did what many groups do. We sang songs while riding down the road. Someone would start singing a song and the rest of us would join in. Finally, the youngest of our group, someone a bit more up on current trends who couldn't stand it any longer, said,

"I've had it!" he shouted. "I can't take it anymore. No one in the car is allowed to sing any song unless it was recorded after 1990!"

"OK," we said, smiling and teasing him just a little. "No problem, let's see here, after 1990, right? Who has a song that was recorded after 1990?"

"I have one," came a voice from the back seat as he began to sing.

"No, that was recorded in the 1980s," a woman in the middle said. "I love that song."

"What about this one?" she took her turn.

"Nope," said our driver, the one who issued the challenge, "1978, and that artist has been dead for fifteen years."

We each took a turn and had no luck. The car went silent except for the occasional few notes as we tried desperately to find a song, one song that was recorded after 1990.

"I give up," one friend said. "I got nothing."

All of us were church folks. A tentative voice said out loud what several in the car were thinking.

"We're trying to get people who weren't even born yet to sing what we were singing in church twenty-five years ago. They may know some of our music, but we don't know any of theirs."

This was an "a-ha" moment, to be sure. We must adapt our worship music to the real, relevant, and relational generations. Our call is away from the culture of predictability and into a culture of freedom to experiment.

Adaptation #7—From Marginal Members to Deep Disciples

Dr. Doug Anderson, Executive Director of the Bishop Rueben Job Center for Leadership Development, has told us that mainline denominational churches in general are better at creating marginal members than making deep disciples of Jesus Christ for the transformation of the world. I believe he is correct.

Believing themselves open to the movement of the Spirit, many congregations have an invitation to Christian discipleship at the end of each worship service. In some traditions, it is an altar call. In mainline traditions, it is more of an invitation to local church membership than an invitation to discipleship. Individuals come forward during the singing of our last service song and present themselves for formal membership.

In the United Methodist tradition, persons promise to uphold the church by their prayers, presence, gifts, service, and witness. This would be bold and outrageous talk if pastors and congregants would take it seriously, but we do not. To honor all five expectations of local church membership would both transform the new members' lives and the church and the world. So why do we look the same after taking those vows? So why does the world look the same?

This email is typical of what passes for an invitation to discipleship: "This is the second Sunday of the month, our 'join the church Sunday.' It is easy to join the church. Simply come forward during the singing of our last service song, answer a few questions from our song book, and have the members greet you in the foyer (or narthex) after the service." Some churches might really knock themselves out by adding something like this: "We will have a four-week class during the Sunday school hour, beginning the first Sunday after Easter. The purpose of this class is to introduce you to our church and let us get better acquainted with you. We hope you will be able to attend."

The inadequacy of this message cannot be overstated. Four weeks to introduce new members to the local church? We hope you will be able to attend? The unspoken message is, "If you are unable to attend, we certainly understand. People are so busy these days. People have so many irons in the fire. We are most grateful you decided to join up with us and look forward to any amount of time, however limited, you might be willing to give to Jesus and this congregation."

Even if this is not said out loud, new people get the message. Think about what has happened to our local churches after decades of receiving marginal members through this process. Since a great number of members are taken in through marginal expectations, it makes sense to assume that they are more than comfortable remaining marginal in their connections to God and Jesus Christ. We have trained them to a dysfunctional culture of very low expectations. Let's look at Matthew 19:16-21 for a deeper understanding:

> A man approached him and said, "Teacher, what good thing must I do to have eternal life?"
>
> Jesus said, "Why do you ask me about what is good? There's only one who is good. If you want to enter eternal life, keep the commandments."
>
> The man said, "Which ones?"

Then Jesus said, "Don't commit murder. Don't commit adultery. Don't steal. Don't give false testimony. Honor your father and mother, and love your neighbor as you love yourself."

The young man replied, "I've kept all these. What am I still missing?"

Jesus said, "If you want to be complete, go, sell what you own, and give the money to the poor. Then you will have treasure in heaven. And come follow me."

Jesus wants our entire lives. We are giving one, maybe two hours per-month. We have a serious disconnect here. How can we be co-creators with God in transforming the world on a one- or two-hour-per month schedule? The culture must adapt from an existing culture of marginal membership into a culture of disciples who transform the world.

Imagine this: We bring our Christian purpose of personal and world transformation into local congregations filled with marginal members. What will the reaction be as our local churches are called into this new culture? What will our members and clergy say? Our members might think: "Hold on there. When I joined up with this outfit, you told me that you were pleased and proud to get me signed on the dotted line. My once-a-month attendance pattern was established. Additionally, I provided evidence that I was adept at deflecting attempts for deeper involvement and participation. You knew this and still you received me into membership. We had an agreement built around marginal membership and now you want to change the contract? I don't think so!"

The movement from marginal membership to deep disciples will be necessary but not necessarily easy. It is a movement from an existing culture of decline into a new culture that is better positioned to live out the purpose of making new disciples of Jesus Christ for the transformation of the world. Here are some things local churches might try:

Elevate local church membership. If now we smile and wink at demanding vows of membership, let us change our tune. No longer is support through prayers, presence, gifts, service, and witness the impossible possibility. Now it is the unvarnished expectation. Clergy and lay leaders will continue to lift up these expectations and others as we build the foundation of accountability for all disciples.

1. Does the new member attend worship every week he or she is in town?

2. Does the new disciple begin with percentage giving and expect to grow into a tithe?

3. Does the new disciple understand that an offering is a contribution beyond a tithe?

4. Does the new disciple pray without ceasing for the local church in ministry?

5. Is the new disciple active in at least one small group outside of worship?

6. Does the new disciple share his or her faith with others?

When we moved west we ran into an unfamiliar practice (to us). We found that in the West it was more common for a local church choir to be given the summer off. One mainline church canceled worship for the entire summer. In this culture, Sunday school was for children only and ran concurrently with worship so as to keep children out of the worship center, keep disruptions to a minimum, and get people out of church in the least amount of time possible. We realized we were trying to implant a high-demand church in which members held one another accountable into a church culture that seemed unfamiliar with holding its membership accountable. As you might guess, declining local churches often live inside low-expectation cultures. Accountability is not achieved by shaming and blaming. It is achieved by telling the truth about high expectations.

Accountability is achieved by telling the truth about high expectations.

"Where have you been, Georgia?" a matriarch of the church community asked. "I have missed you!"

"Well," answered Georgia. "I have been busy."

"Doing what?" asked the church member, genuinely interested in Georgia's life.

"Just this and that," she responded, trying to keep things vague. "There is just not enough time in the day."

"Tell me what is stealing your time," said the woman, unwilling to let Georgia escape further conversation.

"As a single mom, I worry about my daughter, Imogene," replied Georgia, a bit irritated and wanting to avoid what she perceived to be an inquisition. "She is falling behind in reading and she needs extra help. With my work schedule, the only time I have to help her with her reading is Sunday morning, so we have not been able to make it to church."

"That is hard, real hard," the church member said. "You know, I was a single mom myself. I'll keep you in my prayers."

That was the last Georgia ever expected to hear about it. "I'll keep you in my prayers" often means "This conversation is over now, I need to get back to my friends and continue my long-standing church practice of Christian nosiness, which is finding out the business of others and practicing thinly veiled judgment through the expression 'bless her heart.' "

That night, after an exhausted Georgia and Imogene had engaged in tutorial reading warfare, the doorbell rang. On the doorstep there were four women, occupants of the widow's pew at church. Each woman held a casserole in her hands. With the matriarch Georgia had spoken to that morning leading the way, the four women brushed by Georgia and glided into the kitchen.

"Hey, Georgia, hey, Imogene, sweetie," the matriarch shared her greeting. "Georgia, you look tired. Sit down in that chair and prop your feet up. The ladies are putting supper on the table and that will give me just a few minutes to find out from Imogene how we can make reading fun again."

All six had supper together. The four women got to know Imogene better and built a tutoring schedule for the remainder of the month. On a rotating basis, the women would continue to come by and help Imogene with her reading.

After a few weeks, Georgia began to get comfortable enough with the situation to ask questions.

> "Why are you doing this?" Georgia asked after Imogene was tucked in bed for the night.
>
> "Because we have been praying for Jesus to give us some way to live into our faith. I got the feeling that you need us, and we need to be needed. This is not free, you know. We expect something in return."
>
> "Really?" answered Georgia. "What do you want?"
>
> "We need you in church every Sunday. We don't know if you need the church or not, but we need you. We need Imogene in church. We cannot be the church Jesus calls us to be without you both there. If you come, you will help us be who Jesus calls us to be."

Georgia was now ready to fulfill her membership vow of being present in worship every Sunday because those four women were fulfilling their vow of prayers and service. The matriarch demanded accountability from Georgia, which was freely demonstrated. The deep disciple (our matriarch), with her coconspirators, was making a new disciple for Jesus and transforming the world through Imogene, who, even at her young age, realized the need to pay it forward.

When marginal membership is no longer acceptable, it is time to pursue deep discipleship. This path of adaptation means that we transcend our fears and anxieties in order to develop relationships outside our comfort zone. In biblical terms that means we will give our lives for Jesus or take up the cross and follow Jesus. This directive from Jesus is documented in John 13:36-37:

> Simon Peter said to Jesus, "Lord, where are you going?"
> Jesus answered, "Where I am going, you can't follow me now, but you will follow later."
> Peter asked, "Lord, why can't I follow you now? I'll give up my life for you."

And in Matthew 16:24:

> Then Jesus said to his disciples, "All who want to come after me must say no to themselves, take up their cross, and follow me."

Adaptation means that we transcend our fears and anxieties in order to develop relationships outside our comfort zone.

In the story about Georgia, the matriarch develops a relationship with Georgia and her daughter Imogene. In similar examples that follow, Oscar develops a relationship with Roger, and Janet develops a relationship with Ross. These deep disciples showed how all disciples will be known, through loving relationships in the name of Jesus.

Oscar was a new Christian who never did anything halfway. The culture of deep discipleship through relationships fit him. He was a businessman and a numbers guy. He struck up a relationship with an unlikely companion, Roger.

Roger was a loner, likely with untreated mental illness. Roger showed up for meals at the church Oscar had recently joined. Roger never looked anyone in the eye, spoke very few words, and was a compulsive pack rat. Roger had never had a job and had never had any friends. Oscar gave Roger a job cleaning his house, not just because Roger needed the money, which he did, but more important, because Roger needed a friend.

Each week, after Roger did his housekeeper duties, Oscar took him to breakfast. Roger talked, and Oscar listened. After a few months, Roger began to ask for advice, and Oscar shared in return. Roger got a better job and even found a girlfriend; still their conversations continued. These two extraordinarily different men developed a mentor-student relationship.

I asked Oscar how this happened, and he said, "The more I got to know Roger, the more I was involved in his life, the more I liked him." Their relationship was rocky at times, with Roger's untreated mental illness, and Oscar had some issues of his own, but they were intensely loyal to one another. In part, Oscar lived out his deep discipleship through those weekly breakfast conversations with Roger. Oscar, a successful businessman, experienced transformation through his relationship with Roger, a man who happened to be homeless. Oscar did not want to be a marginal member.

Neither did Janet. Janet was a reading specialist for the school system. She was well known in her field. She sang in the church choir, but she wanted something more. In her church she discovered that one of the custodians was illiterate. Ross lived in a different part of town, which might as well have been a different planet. Janet was upper middle class; Ross was one of the working poor. Janet was sophisticated and urbane, while Ross was simple and unpretentious. Janet had a strong self-image, while Ross had low self-esteem.

Janet began to listen to Ross and hear his story. Ross had dreams and goals but he needed the ability to read in order to realize his dreams. Janet spent time before and after choir practice relating to Ross. It is not easy to teach a fifty-year-old man to read, but Janet had a willing heart and spirit. It was an effort that had many starts and stops, but Janet was committed. She went from a marginal member to a deep disciple in the extended time she spent with Ross, helping his dream come to life.

Starting to minister in the safety zone of the local church is the easiest way to begin. After that, branch out into the larger community in which you are located. Meet people where they are, listen to their stories, and build relationships. This can be a difficult, messy business, but it is the path to deep discipleship. It will challenge us to cross socioeconomic, racial, and ethnic lines. If we will take up this cross and follow Jesus in our local churches, we will adapt from being marginal members to deep disciples.

Adaptation #8—From Baby Steps to Giant Leaps

The conventional wisdom for a new, incoming pastor is "Do not change anything in the first year. Learn all you can about the operating culture of the local church and its history before you arrive. Go into the new situation and get to know the people. Let the people know you care. Then after a year, maybe two, you can implement some modest changes, but always remember, baby steps, go slow." This tenet needs adaptation. Here are some ways that problems may emerge when pastors follow that established pattern:

1. After one year of no changes, to initiate healthy, adaptive cultural behaviors may be a shock to the system. The people may have already "settled in" with you. They may be comfortable with no changes and thankful that you have not brought any.

2. It will be more difficult to initiate changes after that first honeymoon year. If the pastor buys in to the current culture of working hard to keep the congregation happy, then to change at the beginning of the second or third year makes the pastor's first-year relationship-building work seem disingenuous.

3. In a sustaining culture of taking baby steps, the people may be happy, but there is no sense of urgency or passion for the purpose of the Christian church.

4. The church no longer has the luxury of baby steps. Critical mass and financial support can decline precipitously over two to three years.

One pastor defied the conventional wisdom of going slowly. The church the pastor served was a local church located adjacent to a large university in a mid-size town. Here is what happened during the pastor's first year.

In July, eight pews were taken out and the remaining pews were repositioned. Prior to this, legroom in the sanctuary was the same as in a Southwest Airlines airplane. The 110 in average attendance moved closer together in a sanctuary that went from a seating capacity of 330 to 250.

In August, two big-screen televisions were purchased for use in adult education programs. The wood floor of the social hall was refinished.

In September, a new young-adult class was started. Also, a new college-age class was started.

In October, the fifty-space parking lot was resurfaced and a "pay station" was installed for public parking income.

"Called to serve" inserts were filled out and returned indicating where God was calling friends and members to serve in ministry.

In November, "pay to park" opened. A worship design team began meeting to explore a new contemporary worship service. A church-wide finance campaign began, introducing a narrative budget. A new leadership committee began work.

In December, the first finance campaign in several years was completed, with increases in numbers of pledging units and total dollars. Church officers were elected, and there were three new young adults in visible leadership positions.

In January, year-end reports revealed that the church had raised a five-year high in dollars for mission. New signage was installed throughout the building for $5,000. A marketing campaign for a new contemporary service with zip-code mailing was started. The new local church website was launched.

In February, the new Sunday morning schedule began, with a 9:00 a.m. contemporary service, 10:00 a.m. Sunday school, and a 11:00 a.m. classic worship service.

In March and April, a food truck was given access to church property for Monday–Friday sales in exchange for providing free food and specialty coffees every Sunday before and after worship.

This was a church on the move. This was a church leader who refused to wait patiently for the right time to take action. The pastor refused to accept delays. Waiting for unanimous decisions is the friend of baby steps and the enemy of giant leaps. One parishioner asked that everyone be brought on board before moving forward.

Waiting for unanimous decisions is the friend of baby steps and the enemy of giant leaps.

"Please," she implored, "let's have a broad-based discussion with everyone in the congregation before we move forward on these things. Let's take a congregation-wide survey and vote on these decisions."

"Please," the pastor answered, "trust your leaders. You elected them to be thoughtful, insightful, and to practice due diligence. The days of baby steps are behind us. If we can adapt to new behaviors now, then we have a chance to thrive."

In order to adapt into a culture where we go from baby steps to giant leaps, we must recognize the urgency of our task. Most of our churches are already on life support. On the practical side, we don't have time for baby steps.

Furthermore, we must recognize what we have become. Smith and Denton, authors of *Almost Christian*, submit that most of our local churches have become practitioners of Moralistic Therapeutic Deism (2010, 14). The guiding beliefs of Moralistic Therapeutic Deism are

1. A God exists who created and orders the world and watches over life on earth.

2. God wants people to be good, nice, and fair to each other, as taught in the Bible and by most religions.

3. The central goal of life is to be happy and to feel good about oneself.

4. God is not involved in lives except when we need God to resolve a problem; God created the world and cares about what happens here. God wants us to be happy, to feel good about ourselves. We are expected to practice biblical rules of being honest, good, and fair. God only intervenes to solve our problems, and rewards us with heaven when we die.

5. Good people go to heaven when they die.

These guiding beliefs are primarily self-serving, and require nothing from us, really. Not only are they totally inadequate as an understanding of the Christian faith, they are not worth being passionate about, much less worth dying for. They are not ideas around which a meaningful life can be built.

Here is a 2012 blog entry from churchfortomorrow.com. This description, from the perspective of the pastor, describes how unfulfilling it can be to attend a church of low expectations.

Week in and week out we watch people come to worship services with low expectations, which are fulfilled. Prayer concerns become a way to peer into the private lives of the neighbors. Printed liturgy becomes a repository for five-syllable words. During the passing of the peace greeting time, the newcomer hears an obligatory "peace of God be with you" from a pew sitter nearby who has no intention of following up this brief exchange with a real conversation after the service, and who immediately turns to more familiar neighbors.

Insider hymns are sung and special music becomes a performance rather than an offering to God. No lives are changed, no new disciples of Jesus Christ are made, and no one takes seriously the possibility of transforming the world. We wonder why the people come. We wonder what keeps them coming back week after week. And of course, one can't help but wonder, what is the point?

That is a description of a worship service in a local church that has low expectations and no urgency or passion. We have become a culture of baby steppers, but we want to complete adaptation into a culture of deep disciples who are able to take giant leaps.

If the purpose to make new disciples for Jesus Christ to transform the world is clear, why wait? Why not now? Why continue to operate in the culture of baby steps when we need a giant leap? We fear that our baby steps have set up too many churches for failure. They make small adjustments, expecting big changes in their growth. When those small steps fail, the resistance to any substantive change at all is only deepened by the failure.

Build relationships. Love the people, but do so in the context of unyielding focus on our purpose as a church. Urgency says "do it now." To be sure, adaptation into new behaviors takes time. Begin now since it may be more than an issue of "can we thrive?" It may go all the way to "can we survive?" In the words of Father Barron: "Paul's message [was] indeed designed to turn the world upside down. . . . If our teaching of the faith is too tepid and uninspiring, authentic Christian proclamation is as subversive and explosive as the earthquake that shook the prison walls in Philippi" (*Catholic Fire*, "Father Barron on Indispensible Men: Peter, Paul, and the Missionary Adventure," Apr. 5, 2011).

The small Texas town of Bastrop had a devastating fire. Hundreds of homes were damaged or destroyed. Local churches prayed for those who were in shock, trying to settle in temporary shelters.

Still others found temporary homes with family or friends. Some victims had insurance, but others did not. Questions swirled around the tragedy.

"How long will it take for the insurance companies to make money available?"

"When will contractors be able to get started and rebuild the homes that were lost?"

"What of those without adequate insurance? Federal disaster relief will be portioned out after mounds of paperwork and will not cover replacement costs."

One denomination in the area began to organize. Meetings were scheduled. People gathered together and talked and prayed for God to find a way through what seemed hopeless. Denominational executives scheduled trips to the area to assess the damage and determine a response. The church folks were all deliberate and cautious. To their credit, the denominational executives wanted to do a good job and wanted to do it right. A baby-steps approach was adopted. More prayers, expert consultants, cost allocation executives, and representatives from ten or more churches talked this thing to death.

One layman disdained baby steps and felt called by God to take a giant leap. "Our church can build one house," he said. He found a family that had no insurance and had lost their home in the fire. Next, he talked with another congregation member who had construction skills. The following Sunday, with the displaced family in attendance at worship, a love offering raised $50,000 to rebuild their modest home. Signup was done through attendance registration pads in the pews and work teams were in place before the sun went down. Everything was ready to go in one week.

"Why not wait and join together in our denomination's effort?" a church representative asked.

"We cannot wait for all the baby steps. We need to take the giant leap now!" was the layman's answer.

Another church in central Texas took a giant leap in their homeless ministry. Desperately poor folks needed work but had no picture identification, a requirement for employment. The catch-22 was that in order to obtain a picture ID, you would need $15. People without jobs often cannot come up with $15. One member of the church suggested that everyone in the congregation should pray about it. Another church member suggested that Christian people establish an ecumenical emergency assistance ministry. In this new ecumenical organization, a committee or task force could be convened to study the issue and pray some more. Within a reasonable amount of time, a plan could be in place and a process established to deal creatively with this issue—tentative, cautious baby steps, when the urgency of the moment cried out for a giant leap! A voice came from across the table:

> "Forget that! These folks need identification now. We have four or five requests each week. The church is short one custodian. I will have the building manager identify four or five jobs each week that can be accomplished in two to three hours. After someone does the job at the church and gets paid, then we will transport them to the Department of Public Safety, where they can get a picture ID and apply for a real job."
>
> "When can we get started?" another in attendance asked.
>
> "Monday of next week. Why wait?"

There was no reason to wait. A sign on the walls of one church in San Francisco reads something like this: "I prayed that God might feed the hungry, clothe the naked, and welcome the stranger and God answered my prayer. God said, 'Do it yourself.'" Answer God's urgent call with giant leaps now. There's no reason to wait.

There's no reason to wait.

Evolutionary theory says that organisms produce more offspring than can survive in order to ensure the continuation of their species. Maybe it follows that Christians produce more local churches than can survive and thrive. Survival of any local church organism is dependent on:

1. Having a strong sense of purpose

2. Adapting (or mutating) to the demands of the environment

3. Discovering a distinctive ministry for the time, place, and history

There is intense competition within most every species, and no one can deny it's true of churches as well. In churches, competition centers on limited resources: money, human capital, priorities in personal life, passion, and commitment. Adaptive local churches will get more than their fair share of these coveted items. It is biblical. Scripture tells us to take giant leaps and eschew the baby steps of anxious and cautious leaders. In the parable of the valuable coins, this recorded summary is attributed to Jesus:

> Those who have much will receive more, and they will have more than they need. But as for those who don't have much, even the little bit they have will be taken away from them. Now take the worthless servant and throw him outside into the darkness. (Matthew 25:29-30)

There was one local church that had great difficulty starting worship on time. When the 11:00 a.m. worship time came each Sunday, only one-third of the eventual attendees had taken their places inside the worship area. The other two-thirds were arriving late from their Sunday school classes or were still out in the halls talking with friends. Church leaders had tried announcements in the bulletin and newsletter, even a plea from the pulpit (odd, since the pulpit announcement was at the beginning of the service and heard by the one-third who were already in the sanctuary), but nothing helped.

The music director and the pastor were concerned. Something had to be done, and the music director had an idea. The next Sunday, the thunderous sound of multiple African, Caribbean, and South American drums came from a distant part of the building. The volume grew as the eight drummers grew closer. Impromptu dancers joined the parade of drummers. The processional traveled through the narthex and into the worship area. Joined by other musicians, the sanctuary filled with God's people and a passionate song of praise filled the space. It was explosive. It communicated the urgency of the task at hand. The expectations were high.

Where does it say that moving the American flag off to the side, or preaching down front, away from the pulpit, are the benchmarks for radical change? Those are baby steps. We need to take a giant leap.

Adaptation #9—From Suspicion to Grace

The culture that assumes people consistently operate out of bad intentions is a culture that is corrosive to the body and incompatible with making new disciples for Jesus Christ. A culture of malice is sustained by suspicious persons who believe that everyone is suspect. A culture of malice believes that all persons want to grab power; no one is above suspicion. Please do not hear what we are not saying. We are not saying that we should be naïve and forget Jesus' admonition to be wise as serpents. We are saying that negative, suspicious people should never be allowed to define our environment or culture (and all churches will attract some of these curmudgeons, because we're the only organization who promises to love them).

Negative, suspicious people should never be allowed to define our environment or culture.

The cultural adaptation from suspicion of others to extending grace to others requires the following adjustments:

1. Trust the community of believers, even though differences exist.

2. Assume the best of intentions, or at least assume honesty until proven otherwise.

3. Assume that we all want to serve Jesus by making disciples for the transformation of the world.

4. Demonstrate willingness to check out assumptions when the behavior of others appears to be a contradiction to faithful discipleship.

For example, local churches in mainline denominations generally have an agreement with the denomination to pay an annual apportionment, a fair-share amount of money to cover that denomination's expenses locally and around the world. Some of these costs cover administration and some of the expenses cover missions. Often there is a furious effort to pay out 100 percent of these apportionments at the end of a calendar year. One parishioner, assuming malice on the part of her pastor, wrote a letter to the denomination's leader that contained the following:

> In the Sunday morning service after Christmas, [our pastors] both misled our congregation regarding our year-end finances. Their statement was "all our debts are paid, all our obligations are met, so all these contributions will go to missions." For many, apportionments are seen as a debt and obligation of the church, and at the time we owed four months' worth of apportionments. While missions may be a part of apportionments, they are not the only source to which apportionment dollars are allocated. [One pastor], compounding the error, appeared before the January meeting of the [church] council and stated that "during the early part of the year, all of our apportionments are directed toward administrative expenses and toward the end of the year, all of our apportionment is paid toward missions." I called [the conference treasurer] and was told that when apportionment payments are received from a church, the money is allocated proportionately to all of the line items that receive money from apportionments.

This section of the letter concludes: "If we cannot believe these ministers on things easily checked out and confirmed, how are we to believe and trust them on matters of faith and spirituality?"

In a culture of grace, a member would read that letter and ask, why would pastors tell parishioners a lie? What's the whole story here?

At the beginning of the financial year, the pastors had asked the denominational treasurer to deviate from historic practices for this particular church and please pay line items for administration before other benevolence line items. The conference treasurer had simply forgotten to do so. What happened was a mistake, rather than deception. The real tragedy is that the parishioner assumed deception, not a mistake.

Further compounding the problem, the parishioner never talked to the pastor prior to writing her letter of complaint to the denomination's leader.

Remember, those who participate in an adaptive culture of grace assume periodic mistakes rather than malice. If one leader recognizes an apparent disconnect between behavior and belief in another, then it will be checked out.

The conversation may go something like this:

"How can you be sure that administrative costs were paid before mission costs?"

"I asked the conference treasurer to do things this way and he agreed," the pastor responds. "He had no problem with it because the end result is the same, and all apportionments are paid in full."

"Why do you think it is better to do it that way?"

"Because missions are more appealing than administration," the pastor confesses, "and when we are begging for money at the end of the year, we want to strengthen our appeal in order to collect all the money we need to end our year in the black."

A culture of suspicion fueled a conflict that could have been easily resolved if the parishioner had extended grace and accepted a simple mistake. The pastor should have put his verbal request in writing at the beginning of the calendar year and sent it to the conference treasurer. The parishioner should have gone directly to the pastor to check things out. This was a mess, and there were no winners.

Some pastors and leaders are not good with details. Rarely is it the case that persons are left off the published prayer list because someone does not like them. If a Sunday morning announcement is forgotten, it is not likely that the one responsible for announcements is punishing that area of ministry responsibility. It is just a mistake, no more, no less.

We've often asked ourselves how suspicious people wind up in leadership in a local church. Why would they be selected? There are, of course, as many answers as there are churches, but an understanding of how small groups function explains part of it. In every small group there are four roles: leader, supportive giver, clown, and critic. All roles are necessary, and no one role is valued over any other role. It is death to the group if there is an overload of any one role at the expense of the others. When there are too many leaders, there is little follow-through. When there are too many supportive givers, there is no vision or direction. When there are too many clowns, the group is without intensity. When there are too many critics, everyone is miserable.

We served a church with what seemed like an overload of critics. There was one laywoman who scoured every piece of printed material put out by the local church. She was good. She could spot mistakes and criticize people for not caring enough "to get it right."

She had a report for us every week:

"You left Barbara off the prayer list this week. I don't think you have ever suffered with a back problem, or you might have been more sensitive to her needs for prayer."

"What happened to the announcement about next week's covered dish? People are not signing up, and we need to know how many people are coming. Do you even care about this fundraiser? It doesn't look like you do."

We had tried to talk with her about how mistakes sometimes happen without any malice or bad intention. She would not budge from the notion that some leaders were working on some hidden agenda and trying to sabotage the efforts of others. Months of her constant and consistent criticism were causing frustration. When anyone tried using reason with her or to explain mistakes, their efforts were ineffectual.

In the face of her criticism the pastor opted to adapt their somber interaction into a playful invitation. The opportunity, or test, came less than one week after this new resolve.

"I saw in the bulletin yesterday that there was no listing of our lay leader and governing board chair. We have always listed these offices in the bulletin every week in case people might want to contact leaders with a concern about what is happening at the church. Why did you leave them off?"

"I just wanted to see if you would notice," the pastor replied with a smile in her direction. "You are the most observant member we have. Keep watching, because each week we are going to omit something from the bulletin. We may put in a new phrase or we may just leave it blank. We are going to run a tally. This will fit perfectly with your skill set. You are the best I have ever seen at finding errors!"

To everyone's surprise, that was the last critique we heard from this church member. Maybe she continued her critique somewhere else, but her weekly reports listing all the mistakes of the past week were over.

All church leaders have a lot of things on their minds each Sunday morning and sometimes they (we) just plain forget. These are mistakes. There is no malice in them. The local church can cultivate an environment of grace with forgiveness for mistakes rather than resorting to accusations and animosity.

Adaptation #10—From a Generic Culture to a Self-Defined Culture

The last of the critical adaptations in culture is moving from a generic local church culture to a self-defined community. What do we mean by a *generic church culture?* Many new expressions of community-based churches are in fact trying to appeal to all faiths. They regard all faith teachings as equally true and do not prioritize one over another. However, when a Christian church adopts this generic culture, they have lost their own self-definition. In a generic church culture, the majority of members would agree with these statements:

"It doesn't matter what you believe, as long as you believe."

"All churches are the same no matter where you go."

"Every religion follows the golden rule: 'Do unto others as you would have them do unto you.' Therefore, all religions are the same."

"Christians should accept everyone and not exclude anyone from church."

Many Christians, both progressive and evangelical, say things like this. It is the generic, or "all-inclusive," package, which is meant to communicate that everything goes here. To the extent that this is the case with any church, this assumption is not only untrue but also the all-inclusive culture that could destroy a local church.

Early on in ministry, a pastor made a huge mistake. The pastor asked an individual who was intelligent, knowledgeable, affable, and personable to teach an adult Sunday school class. This newly appointed teacher paid close attention to guests in the class and had the gift of gathering; people wanted to be with him. He was excellent at involving everyone in class discussions. He knew more about the Bible and biblical research than most seminary graduates. Because of this, the class grew in number and was popular. The teacher was simply a great guy. There was just one problem. He was a self-described agnostic. He saw no evidence of the existence of God.

The class demonstrated a tolerance for diverse opinions with every topic. It became a class of "it doesn't matter what you believe just as long as you believe." Word spread throughout the community that this was a church that followed Buddha and Mohammed with the same passion as Jesus. We were thought to be "open" and filled with progressive interfaith thought. The local church was accepting of everything, defined by nothing. They were in muddy waters.

The effective teacher came to the pastor and said,

"I need to turn in my resignation as teacher for the class."

"Why would you do that?" asked the pastor.

"Because," he explained, "at this time in my life, I don't believe in Jesus as Lord."

"But that is such a tricky thing," the pastor replied, worrying more about coverage for the class the next Sunday than adherence to such a primary statement of faith for the historic church. "Remember that 'Jesus is Lord' was as much a reaction by early believers to the oppressive Roman rule insisting on Caesar as Lord. Then there is the question of sexism of the word 'Lord' and how many scholars recognize this language as off-putting to women who seek faith."

"You are not hearing me," the teacher interrupted. "I understand what you are saying, but you must know, there is a problem for any Christian church that has a Sunday school teacher who does not believe Jesus is Lord. That is basic."

Do not mistake what we are saying. "Jesus is Lord" does not mean the same thing to all Christians, but hopefully all Christians can find personal meaning in the statement "Jesus is Lord." From that moment forward, the local church began to closely examine what they wanted to instill in worship attendees as well as what they wanted in their local church leaders. Congregations cannot live out of generic church at the expense of our own self-definition.

How do we continue to challenge the notion that our local churches can be all-inclusive? How do we challenge the perception that our local church can be all things to all people? Not everyone desires to be a Jesus follower. The church has a specific purpose of making disciples of Jesus for the transformation of the world. The church cannot do every possible good thing. The church must do its one good thing. The following three questions help any local church maintain an openness to everyone while at the same time maintaining alignment with the purpose of all churches.

If not a believer in Jesus Christ, are you a seeker? In other words, do you seek a closer connection with God?

If not a seeker, then are you respectful of the local church's purpose and self-definition? In other words, if not a seeker, will you step back and not get in the way of those who are seekers?

Along with deep disciples, do you assume that God is not through with you yet? In other words (John Wesley's), are you moving on to perfection?

The generic church is a slippery slope in another way as well. Once we buy in to the idea that we must welcome and accept all belief systems, then it is a short ride to accepting any and all kinds of behavior as well.

The church cannot do every possible good thing.

For example, we served a local church that had become welcoming of persons from every background, as well as persons facing a variety of challenges. Many of our regular attendees were addicted to various substances; others were living with various forms of mental illness from mild to severe. All of them were expected to be able to maintain a minimum standard of self-regulation. Panhandling was forbidden, as were any outbursts, threats, or behavior that would frighten others.

Not connected with this influx of newcomers, there was one longtime member whose behavior had long been tolerated by the church body. As an example, she made a practice of using the *N* word to identify persons of color, demanded that anyone who sat in her regular seat in our sanctuary move at once, and hit children with her cane if they passed too closely. The leadership talked about it.

"What are we going to do with Myrtle?" someone opened the conversation. "She can't behave like that in church!"

"That's just how Myrtle is," answered another leader. "She has had a difficult life."

"I have sympathy for her circumstances," still another leader joined in, "but Myrtle has consistently run off anyone who sits near her. I have friends who visited, but after their experiences with Myrtle, they won't come back."

"But what of our Christian obligation to love everyone just as they are? It is doubtful that Myrtle will ever change," a group member reminded us. She desperately wanted to save Myrtle and save her church.

"Here is an idea," someone proposed. "If we had three or four persons who were gifted in helping others self-regulate, they could take turns sitting with Myrtle each Sunday. Perhaps she could stop the racist language, the demands, and using her cane as a weapon if someone was glued to her side the whole time she was in the building."

"Where are we going to find four people to do that?" came a concerned voice.

"Maybe we can't," answered the one who made the proposal, "but we should pray that God will send us four who would be willing to share in this unusual ministry."

"And if God does not answer our prayers in a timely way?" one man asked with a twinkle in his eye.

"Then we fall back on our cardinal rule. Do everything possible to be in ministry to all of God's people. If the behavior of the one continues to be destructive to the community as a whole, then we must ask that one to leave rather than allow damage to the body of Christ."

God sent three persons who had the necessary gifts. For four weeks someone sat with Myrtle, loved on her, and insisted that she practice self-regulation during her time of worship. Not unexpectedly, Myrtle felt this new expectation of her worship behavior to be confining. By the fifth week, Myrtle was a no-show, and she never returned to church after that.

We got word that Myrtle moved into a nursing home facility soon after she stopped coming to our church. This living facility was better able to help Myrtle self-regulate, and the new worshiping community had other residents growing in the grace of self-regulation opportunities just like Myrtle.

We never cease to be amazed at the behavior that is tolerated in many local churches. From a choir member throwing hymnals to a member who in anger shouted four-letter words at the pastor at an Easter morning brunch—both true stories! Not everyone can self-regulate. Yes, we promise that God loves them, and that we will, too. But loving people does not mean we must tolerate behavior that is destructive to the church. Being inclusive isn't forgetting who we are as Christians. As pastors and leaders, it is our job to set expectations, to provide self-definition, and to ask that every member's behavior serves to build up and not tear down. When someone consistently violates expectations, then loving steps need to be taken. Whether it is relieving a Sunday school teacher or assigning a chaperone to hold accountable someone with unregulated behavior, this is consistently and honestly living out our self-definition.

Part Four

The Culture of Transformation

A team from one local church was assigned the task of describing the movement from an old, familiar way of doing church into a new, purpose-centered way of worshiping. The pastor set the stage for this conversation with a scripture passage familiar to the great majority of leaders in the local church:

> Jesus entered Jericho and was passing through town. A man there named Zacchaeus, a ruler among tax collectors, was rich. He was trying to see who Jesus was, but, being a short man, he couldn't because of the crowd. So he ran ahead and climbed up a sycamore tree so he could see Jesus, who was about to pass that way. When Jesus came to that spot, he looked up and said, "Zacchaeus, come down at once. I must stay in your home today." So Zacchaeus came down at once, happy to welcome Jesus.
>
> Everyone who saw this grumbled, saying, "He has gone to be the guest of a sinner."
>
> Zacchaeus stopped and said to the Lord, "Look, Lord, I give half of my possessions to the poor. And if I have cheated anyone, I repay them four times as much."
>
> Jesus said to him, "Today, salvation has come to this household because he too is a son of Abraham. The Human One came to seek and save the lost." (Luke 19:1-10)

"I have read this story more times than I can remember," began the pastor, "but today I read it truly, for the first time. It was the first time I saw, really noticed, verse five. When Jesus reached the spot where Zacchaeus was, Jesus 'looked up.' Jesus would never have noticed Zacchaeus, never known he was there, unless he took the time to look up."

The pastor identified the need for the congregation to move

from a culture that keeps its head buried in familiar relationships to a culture that looks up to see the least, last, and lost.

"This means adapting to a new culture," he said. "This means moving outside our comfort zones."

Another team member then rose and identified the existing local church culture around worship.

"I asked several of our church folks to answer the question 'Why I come to worship.' Here is my report."

Many of the church folks reported that they came to church to sing the grand hymns of our faith. One person said it this way: "I remember attending church with my grandfather when I was very young. My grandfather was a tentmaker Southern Baptist pastor and served a small rural church. I was amazed at the singing. My grandfather never opened a hymnal. He knew all the words by heart. As I watched him sing it was clear that these hymns meant a great deal to him. I don't know if it was the melodies or the lyrics, but the hymns brought peace to his spirit. Even as a child, I knew I wanted some of that. I come to church searching for that feeling and keeping my grandfather's memory alive."

Another person shared, "I come to church because of the beauty of the architecture. I love these stained glass windows. I see the biblical stories that are told through the stained glass. This space is the most sacred space on earth for me. It is the place where God lives. I come to God's house to be close to God."

"I come to worship for quiet prayer," said another, inspired by the personal stories pouring out from long-term members. "Prayer is at the center of my faith life. It is my conversation with God. The best conversation is when I stop talking and listen to God. I pray for myself, and I enjoy hearing concerns from the community so I can pray for others."

There were other responses reported out from this team leader. "I come to church to hear a good sermon. I need some help getting through the week, and often a good word from the preacher will start my week off right."

"I think worship is a good place to be for moral maintenance," still one more reported. "I want to live a good, ethical, and moral life, and attending church on Sunday helps me make it happen."

Last, someone reported, "I come to church to see my friends. My week is hectic. I work in a cubicle in a high-rise office. I don't have much interaction with my coworkers and I live alone, so church becomes the place where I can catch up with my friends. I look forward to it."

All these comments speak to the church culture that was built in the twentieth century. These are familiar ways in which we do church. Congregations that do church live in a culture that is recognizable to all of us. But what if we transitioned from a culture of doing church into a new culture where people were determined to be the church? Worship would be one of the first things that would change:

As believers come up the walkway that leads into the worship space, their hearts are filled with a passion for Jesus. People are coming to church because they love Jesus Christ. People are coming to worship because Jesus was and still is alive. Worship is the celebration place where Jesus is lifted up as our window and pathway to connect with God.

Throughout the worship experience believers can readily see that every ministry is done for the transformation of the world. Our world is a mess, and Jesus provides a radical intervention that will transform the world. We pray out loud, "Thy kingdom come, thy will be done, on earth as it is in heaven." We expect the kingdom of God to come on earth. John the Baptist may have preached that the kingdom of God was coming, but Jesus called us to live in the kingdom of God on earth today.

It follows that the kingdom of God lived out on earth by people transformed in Jesus will take shape through relationships. Living our lives through the lens of Matthew 25:40, we will look for Jesus' face in those we meet. In worship every Sunday, we will look on the faces of people, friends and strangers alike, and see the face of Jesus. We will seek new relationships because every person opens up for us new possibilities for our own transformation as we strive to grow in understanding and connection to God.

Now it makes sense when we say our purpose out loud: to make new disciples of Jesus for the transformation of the world. We are called to listen, love, and be present with those who are known by

God but are strangers to us, and God may be a stranger to them. We model in our behavior what it means to put love, as Jesus loves, in action wherever we find ourselves. One great opportunity to live out the love of Jesus is when we worship together.

The bottom line is we are called to move from doing church to being the church. What does it matter if we sing, pray, and practice high moral behavior if we have yet to be transformed by Jesus? We are the new creation. This is not an old culture with simple correctives and adjustments. Worship is not to be filled with helpful hints for hurtful habits. Inside this new culture we live Jesus' words found in Mark 12:30, "you must love the Lord your God with all your heart, with all your being, with all your mind, and with all your strength."

We are called to move from doing church to being the church.

Churches Can Practice Variance

In the same way that not all finches are alike, not all churches are alike. Christians will adapt to their unique ministry setting over time as an act of faithfulness and calling, just like species adapt over time to their unique environments.

Local churches have a lifecycle. They are born, they grow, plateau, and if they don't experience a rebirth during the plateau phase, they enter into decline and eventually die. In the same way, some species will die out, or go extinct, while others will be formed anew. We can see evidence for this in many areas of the country. In the best of circumstances, one local congregation will go extinct and a different, adaptive congregation will take over that site. The congregation going out has failed to adapt its culture, while the one coming in is growing and thriving because its attempts at adaptation have been successful.

In the worst of circumstances, the once-proud church building is sold to become a restaurant or wine bar. Entrepreneurs keep close tabs on shifts in cultural tastes, as well as staying up with the leading edge on local real estate markets. Maybe boutique restaurants are able to capture a Sunday brunch crowd when local churches of the area have become irrelevant in the same location. Either way, a local church dies because it cannot adapt. But there is hope.

> So now, prophesy and say to them, The LORD God proclaims: I'm opening your graves! I will raise you up from your graves, my people, and I will bring you to Israel's fertile land. You will know that I am the LORD, when I open your graves and raise you up from your graves, my people. I will put my breath in you, and you will live. I will plant you on your fertile land, and you will know that I am the LORD. I've spoken, and I will do it. This is what the LORD says. (Ezekiel 37:12-14)

The struggle of adaptation will happen not only between species but also between individuals within the same species. In the same way, the struggle of adaptation will not only be between denominations but also between individual local churches.

Since organisms pass genetic traits on to their offspring (Dr. Edwin Friedman said congregations have distinctive DNA), dying churches pass "dying genes" in the form of church culture to their dwindling numbers. That is how organisms go extinct. Dying churches tend to replicate themselves with transfer of members and these declining cultural behaviors, which compound their dwindling numbers. Some would argue that is not such a bad thing because this inevitable extinction opens up niches that will be colonized (evangelized) by a new group of Christians. On the other hand, vibrant, healthy churches that know and practice their purpose will pass on their life genes to new and passionate Christians.

Vibrant, healthy churches that know and practice their purpose will pass on their life genes to new and passionate Christians.

In evolutionary parlance, this struggle of adaptation is called variance. Variance occurs in the natural world primarily in one of two ways: through changing the genetic code, or through changes in the environment. In modern times, we can and have experimented with many kinds of variance. Do you recall the whippet, a new dog breed formed by combining the genetic material of both a greyhound and a terrier? It is time that congregations learned how to do their own genetic engineering. Let's consider a few examples of congregations that either chose or were forced to become a new breed because of their new culture.

In the center city of a major metropolitan area, there was a local church that had had a long and distinguished life. As their worship numbers shrank and their median age rose, a few local church leaders recognized that this venerable congregation was headed for extinction unless there was a dramatic intervention. The congregation cried scarcity of resources; they were somber in their life together, predictable in their worship, and unforgiving about mistakes. The congregation ignored its neighbors and was reluctant to practice transparency.

In order to thrive, the congregation would have to widen its appeal on various fronts (variance).

This congregation decided to go the way of the whippet.

The local church, using the principle of variance, became a new breed itself. They first developed an extensive ministry to persons who were without shelter and living in the downtown area. There were over three thousand homeless persons downtown each day, so this seemed to be a natural choice for mission. At the same time, the local church became the center for the city's symphony as well. A city concert hall was only one block away, and musicians would practice inside the church all the time. When the concert hall was unavailable, the symphony would perform in the church. Several members of the symphony formed a chamber ensemble that played primarily in the local church sanctuary during one of the services.

Still not satisfied with the level of diversity in ministry, the church began a new worship service with jazz music. It was filled with the city's best jazz musicians and attracted an entirely different group of aficionados. When the major jazz figure in the city died, the funeral was held in this church. Symphony members volunteered to serve meals to homeless persons in the church as well as to teach disadvantaged folks how to play various instruments. On one occasion, there was an advent choir made up entirely of poor and marginalized persons from the area. The best news of this new breed of church is that persons from radically different walks of life came to be in relationship with each other.

The few visionary church leaders realized that cultural adaptation could come on many fronts. The local church had to adapt itself to all downtown life. They began to pay attention to diversity and creativity. One specific thing would not ensure survival.

Sometimes church leaders initiate giant leaps in ministry, while other times the ministry explodes around them. The point is, the future belongs to God. Sometimes we are only along for the ride as our cultural adaptations are forced on us. Heather Heinzman Lear reported this story about a local church in Antioch, Tennessee: Even without invitation, the neighbors decided to be in relationship with this particular local church. Now the church had to do something but what would they do? Some were too anxious to act. Some could not break out of their comfort zone. Others, however, were brave and bold. The new Egyptian neighbors became a part of the local church community. Transportation was an issue so the church purchased a bus to help out the newest members of their community. Parents needed help in child rearing and learning conversational English so the church pitched in to make these things happen. Worship services in the Egyptian language became a staple of church life. . . . These were not people who necessarily chose adaptative change for themselves but embraced adaptation when it was thrust on them ("Welcoming New Neighbors," GBOD, *Romans 12 Newsletter*, Issue #162, 2013).

One thing we have learned from the Darwinian notion of natural selection is that those organisms who change are more likely to survive and reproduce. The stories of these two churches are stories of variance. They are stories of healthy and passionate, deep disciples using their adaptive powers in order to survive and reproduce.

121

How Will We Know?

Churches that fail to adapt will continue to pass on dying genes to all who embrace their outdated culture. Because none of these adaptations are likely to come easily to a church, adaptation for congregations must be intentional and deliberate. As the whippet was not produced by accident, so adaptation of this sort will not happen unless we identify, research, plan, execute, and measure. If a local church is asking the following questions (or measuring the following items), it is a signal that there has been little necessary adaptation to a new culture:

How many times have we sung our favorite hymns in worship?

How much time does our pastor spend in her office?

How many different causes are honored at our church?

Who are the biggest givers?

How many members do we have on the rolls?

These are not the questions of a new organism. These are questions of accountability, but these questions do not measure what is necessary for survival. New organisms are focused on doing the actions that will ensure a future. The following questions are examples of measuring those factors that will contribute to survival:

What is our first-time visitor traffic each Sunday?

How many people do we have in worship attendance?

How many active small groups do we have in our church?

How many new disciples have been made through baptism and professions of faith?

Do our members know our purpose?

It is easy to see how these questions are in alignment with the purpose of making new disciples of Jesus for the transformation of the world. Adapting to a new culture will mean that these questions take priority over institutional support questions. Answering these last questions helps church leaders measure the stuff that matters.

Epilogue

All movements tend to follow a predictable pattern. A respected denominational leader identified the lifecycle of all movements in this way: "A visionary starts the movement, the movement grows, and stabilizes, is institutionalized and is recognized as productive. At that point the movement experiences unrecognized decline, then recognized decline, and will either die or experience an apostolic vision again" (personal conversation with author [Karen]).

Most denominations and local churches are either in unrecognized or recognized decline. Most local churches will either go extinct or adapt and thrive. We do have a choice here. Guided by our purpose, healthy genes, adaptation of culture, and variance possibilities, we will become a new kind of church. With us or without us, it will happen.

One of the great biblical stories from Ezekiel gives us hope for adaptation:

> The LORD's power overcame me, and while I was in the LORD's spirit, he led me out and set me down in the middle of a certain valley. It was full of bones. He led me through them all around, and I saw that there were a great many of them on the valley floor, and they were very dry. He asked me, "Human one, can these bones live again?"
>
> I said, "LORD God, only you know."
>
> He said to me, "Prophesy over these bones, and say to them, Dry bones, hear the LORD's word! The LORD God proclaims to these bones: I am about to put breath in you, and you will live again. I will put sinews on you, place flesh on you, and cover you with skin. When I put breath in you, and you come to life, you will know that I am the LORD."
>
> I prophesied just as I was commanded. There was a great noise as I was prophesying, then a great quaking, and the bones came together, bone by bone. When I looked, suddenly there were sinews on them. The flesh appeared, and then they were covered over with skin.

But there was still no breath in them.

He said to me, "Prophesy to the breath; prophesy, human one! Say to the breath, The LORD God proclaims: Come from the four winds, breath! Breathe into these dead bodies and let them live."

I prophesied just as he commanded me. When the breath entered them, they came to life and stood on their feet, an extraordinarily large company. (Ezekiel 37:1-10)

Local churches do not need to become extinct. With the breath of God we can and will become new again. We will be planted on fertile land. Maybe that will be a new geographic locale, but more likely it will not be geography that changes. The difference will be in remembering who we belong to and aligning with our purpose. We cannot survive or thrive unless we go where the breath of God takes us.

Appendix

Part 1 Organizations, Organisms, and Cultural Identity

If you had to describe your congregation as a person, how would you describe him or her?

Gender _____ Age _____

Personality (circle those that apply, or write in other):

Outgoing, extroverted
Introverted, interested mostly in ideas and/or theology
Friendly
Reserved
Shy
Flexible
Easy to know
Other:

_____
_____
_____
_____

Likes and dislikes:

Music
Drama and theater
Reading
Study (what kind)
Parties and play

Other:

_____

_____

_____

_____

Other interests:

_____

_____

_____

_____

Fears, hopes, and dreams:

_____

_____

_____

_____

(Share in small groups or pairs, depending on size of group.)

Adaptation (share in small groups)

1. What adaptations have you made in your own life? (Eg, marriage, children, moving, extended family, work, etc.)

_____

_____

_____

_____

2. What is your congregation's stated purpose? What do you see as the central purpose of the Christian Church?

_____

_____

_____

_____

3. List some examples of adaptations in the Hebrew Scriptures and in the New Testament. (Work from your own knowledge of the Bible; the passages listed below will get you started.)

Adam and Eve   Jesus in hometown synagogue
Joseph in Egypt   Feeding of the five thousand
Israelites in Egypt   Peter's dream
Israel in the wilderness   Church in Corinth
King David   Acts 2
The exile of Israel   Jesus' healing stories

4. How are you different because you are a Christian? How much of your identity comes from your family? Your work? Your faith?

_____

_____

_____

_____

5. What is the biggest barrier or obstacle for you in sharing your faith with others?

_____

_____

_____

_____

Part 2 Adapt to Your Unique Environment

Using the description you wrote of your congregation as a person, discuss how you believe your congregation appears to your community and whether or not that image is different from the community's own identity. (Ideally, each participant would do some informal research about this before attending.)

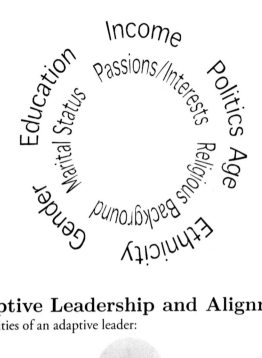

Income
Passions/Interests
Politics
Education
Marital Status
Age
Religious Background
Gender
Ethnicity

Adaptive Leadership and Alignment
Qualities of an adaptive leader:

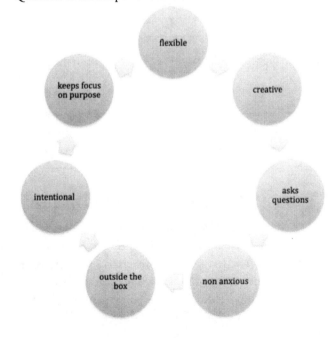

flexible

keeps focus on purpose

creative

intentional

asks questions

outside the box

non anxious

See if you can come up with antonyms for each of these qualities. The opposite of these qualities will result in a church that struggles with adapting to its environment. Not only do leaders need these qualities but the practice of these behaviors will create a powerful atmosphere or culture for healthy adaptation.

Identify which of these qualities comes easiest to you, which ones you might be able to develop, and which qualities you will need to depend on other team members to provide.

Strategize on how you will address the situation when the qualities that stifle adaptation arise. Discuss with your leadership team, and covenant together to create the atmosphere of healthy adaptation. (This covenant needs to include a way to address behaviors that stifle adaptive leadership. This might be a healthy role for the "critic" in the group, but staying on track has to be the job of all leadership, not just a select few.)

Alignment

1. Brainstorm a list of common church activities, programs, events, and ministries.

2. Using the purpose "Make disciples of Jesus Christ for the transformation of the world," identify the activities that directly accomplish the purpose, indirectly accomplish the purpose, and do not connect to the purpose. For each item that "indirectly accomplishes the purpose," indicate the pathway of connection back to the purpose itself.

3. Survey the whole, looking for what portion of your church's activities directly relate to the above purpose.

4. Align these ministries/events in reference to the church's use of financial resources and people resources.

5. Ask these questions:

131

What percentage of your ministries are directly related to the purpose?

What percentage of your budget is directly related to the purpose?

What percentage of your people are directly related to the purpose?

Often this exercise in itself will illuminate why a church has either plateaued or declined. Discuss how better alignment could be practiced in your local church setting.

Part 3 The Culture of Transformation

Cultural Adaptations from Scarcity to Abundance

1. Growing up, how open was your family about money? Did your parents tithe? Did they talk to you about it? Did you tithe yourself as a child? Did you receive an allowance?

2. Who knows how much money you make? Employer? Other employees? Spouse? Children? Parents? Friends? How do they know? How comfortable are you discussing money?

3. Discuss Mt. 6:2-4; Mt. 19:23-24; Acts 2:41-47 and how they apply to us today.

4. Looking at your own checkbook or credit card statements, where does most of your money go? What percentage of your income do you give away?

5. Discuss why it is that people at the middle and lower end of the economic scale give away a greater percentage of their income than upper-income people give.

6. How many months operating expenses does your church have

saved in a foundation or otherwise set aside? Do you feel it is too much or too little?

7. What assets does your church have that may be untapped? How entrepreneurial do you think your church is willing to be?

8. In a few sentences, describe how you believe God views money.

_____

_____

_____

_____

From Entitlement to Egalitarianism

1. None of us like to imagine ourselves as entitled, yet undoubtedly we all feel entitled to something. See if you can identify anything you feel you are entitled to have or to receive (things or privileges you take for granted).

_____

_____

_____

_____

2. Imagine how entitlement may have functioned in the first century church. Using these passages as a guide, identify the issues of entitlement at work. (See 1 Cor. 1:10-16; Acts 10:34-43; Acts 11:17-22; Acts 12: 14-18; Acts 17:1-8; Gal. 1:11-14; Gal. 3:27-29). Then translate these issues from the first century into today's church culture.

From Somberness to Playfulness

1. "Somber is the ally of perfection." Explain and interpret this statement in light of your church's practice of worship.

2. As a group, try to distinguish between reverent atmosphere and a somber atmosphere.

3. On a scale of one to ten, rank these elements of your worship services for their degree of spontaneity. (One—least spontaneity; ten—most spontaneity.)

> a. liturgy
> b. prayer
> c. music
> d. sermon or message
> e. children's time
> f. readings
> g. other activities?

4. Identify the elements of your worship that would lend to more playfulness.

5. Do the same exercise with your meetings, informal gatherings, and so forth.

6. How much time does your church allot to just having fun together?

From Limited Access to Trust

1. Who has keys to your church's property?

2. How are the decisions made regarding who is given keys and who is not? (A function of the church office? Other?)

3. Make a list of the advantages and disadvantages of broad access to church property.

Boundaries are a necessary, healthy part of life. They define use and misuse, ownership, responsibility, among other things. One healthy purpose of boundaries is to clarify expectations and create respect. What other health purposes of boundaries can you identify?

Boundaries also have a way of establishing a level of fear and anxiety, should the boundaries be violated. Discuss where you have witnessed or experienced this (church sanctuaries, a shop with many breakable objects, "no skateboarding" signs, "no loitering" signs, etc.).

How do boundaries affect the practice of hospitality in a church? in a home?

How could property be protected from abuse or misuse but still be freely used by church and community?

From Ignoring the Neighbors to Embracing the Neighbors

Using the table from part 2, to what degree are your church members different from the individuals in the community where your church is located? Of the items listed below, which ones do you think form the greatest barrier to connecting with the community, in the minds of church members?

Age	Gender	Income level
Education	Politics	Ethnicity
Language	Marital Status	Passions/interests
Religious Background		

Which of the above items do you think might be seen by the community as differences that keep them from participating in your church?

Select two or three items to work with. Discuss why the item is a barrier. With each item seen as a barrier, identify two or three ways a church could address the barrier and change the participation. For example, if the income level of church attenders is higher than income level of those living in the neighborhood, the community might feel they would not experience a sense of belonging in the church.

Sometimes we assume something is a barrier, but the community doesn't even know enough about our church to think that barrier exists. This means the barrier exists in our minds, in our culture. It is the way we perceive the neighborhood, not the other way around. Sometimes a barrier exists only in perception, and not in reality. Decide if this applies to any of the differences you've identified so far.

End by affirming that Jesus routinely told stories about overcoming barriers and sometimes is the one who breaks down barriers by being the bridge himself. Identify a series of Scripture passages that illustrate this point. (E.g., woman caught in adultery; healing of Jairus's daughter; the Samaritan woman; Zaccheus; the man by the pool; the tenth leper; the woman who anointed his feet with oil.)

From Predictability to Freedom

1. What are the most predictable elements of your worship services:

Order	Singing
Service music	Sermons
Readings	Greeting
Liturgy	Prayers
What's on the screen	Announcements
Ushers	Sacraments

2. Give examples of how each element could move from predictability to freedom.

3. How rigid are the roles and activities in your church?

Only the pastor does the funerals or speaking in worship
Our ushers all have tenure
We have a group who rotate among the various committees
We don't rotate our church officers
We have the same events seasonally (Easter, Christmas, Lent, etc.)
In worship, we always have _____
In meetings, we always _____
In fellowship, we always _____

4. How often do leaders say, "We've tried that before"?

New people bring new ideas. It sounds too obvious to need stating, yet it is again and again a stumbling block for churches. If the "new people" want to have glow sticks on Christmas Eve instead of candlelight, how is that received? How do new people respond if their ideas aren't allowed to shape the congregation's life?

From Marginal Members to Deep Disciples

Working in small groups, see if you can define the vows or expectations of membership for your congregation. For each item, quantify how often (weekly, daily, 10 percent, 5 percent, whatever you can do is fine, etc.).

Attendance
Study
Giving
Service or mission
Witness

Have each person write their answer down on their own first, without discussion. When comparing your answers, note the differences and with what ease or difficulty is experienced in clarifying and reaching an agreement.

A church's general membership will never fulfill their church vows to a greater degree than the leadership itself fulfills the vows. To what degree is your church's leadership in agreement about what it means to be a member? Are there any considerations given in the nominating process to a leader's fulfillment of their church vows?

If and when an agreement is reached, discuss how this is communicated to the church's membership and potential members without seeming legalistic.

Discuss the role of accountability in the Christian life. Is there a danger to the practice of accountability and if so, what is the danger?

Is there a danger in a lack of accountability, and if so, what is the danger?

From Baby Steps to Giant Leaps

Some church leaders believe that churches are particularly "change resistant." Do you agree? If so, why do you think this might be?

What are advantages and disadvantages of going slow with regard to introducing change in a local church?

Define the "consensus method" of group decision making. What are its advantages and disadvantages? Do you think consensus should be the predominant decision-making method used in churches and why or why not?

Some churches complain that pastors or leaders try to change things too fast. What rate of change do you think would be needed for your local church to catch up to today's world, culturally and technologically?

If you could select five important changes for your church's future to be undertaken in the next year, what would they be? How would you implement those changes? What do you imagine the response might be?

From Suspicion to Grace

None of us like the experience of being mistrusted, but in a church body the experience can be especially destructive. Insofar as you are comfortable, and without identifying anyone, share an experience where the trust between you and someone else was broken or damaged. Was the relationship mended, and if so, how? If not, what happened to the situation over time?

See if your small group can differentiate between constructive criticism and character assassination. Imagine you are writing behavior guidelines to be used by program ministry committees and the personnel committee at your church. (Be as specific as possible.)

Case Study—2 Corinthians

Discuss 2 Corinthians as a case study of moving from a culture of suspicion to a culture of grace. Particularly note these passages: 2 Cor. 1:8-14; 15-24; 2 Cor. 2:1-10; 2 Cor. 4:7-12; 2 Cor. 5:16-21; 2 Cor. 10:7-11.

We have probably lost one of Paul's letters, but reading between the lines, what do you think might have happened on Paul's previous visit to Corinth?

Do you think Paul appears defensive? Why or why not?

Where do you see words of comfort in his reply?

Where do you see words of challenge in his reply?

How do both comfort and challenge help us to move from suspicion to grace?

Paul challenges us to be ambassadors of reconciliation. How does he tell us to do that? How would you embody that behavior today?

From a Generic Culture to a Self-Defined Culture

1. How does a church adapt to the surrounding culture without losing its identity and/or self-definition?

2. How does your church define the essentials of its faith?

3. Read Acts 17:16-31 for Paul's famous sermon in Athens, Greece. How does Paul try to connect with his listeners?

4. How does he adapt the gospel to his listeners?

5. What does he lift up in the sermon as the essentials of the faith?

6. To what degree can essentials of the faith be different to different hearers?

7. Are there elements or beliefs in the Christian faith that are non-negotiable for you? for your church?

8. What makes these practices or ministries Christian and not secular? In other words, what sets them apart?

> A preschool
> An exercise class
> A sports team
> A study of any non-Bible book
> Meditation
> A covered dish dinner or sharing a meal
> Marriage or parenting classes

A Culture of Transformation

1. What does the transition from "doing" church to "being" church mean to you?

2. Which of the ten cultural adaptations have your church successfully managed?

3. Which future cultural adaptations might your congregation be receptive to?

The DNA of a church is a product of its past history as well as its present culture. It includes strengths as well as weaknesses. DNA indicates tendencies and preferences, as well as aversions and avoidances. Based on knowledge of your church and its history, see if you can identify some markers of your church's DNA.

CPSIA information can be obtained at www.ICGtesting.com
Printed in the USA
LVOW05s0703090314

376495LV00004B/4/P

9 781426 773037